Patrick White

Twayne's World Authors Series
Australian Literature

Joseph Jones, Editor
University of Texas, Austin

TWAS 711

PATRICK WHITE
Photograph by John Stockdale, 1979
Courtesy of Jonathan Cape, London

Patrick White

By John A. Weigel
Miami University

Twayne Publishers • Boston

Patrick White

John A. Weigel

Copyright © 1983 by G. K. Hall & Company
All Rights Reserved
Published by Twayne Publishers
A Division of G. K. Hall & Company
70 Lincoln Street
Boston, Massachusetts 02111

Book Production by John Amburg

Book Design by Barbara Anderson

Printed on permanent/durable acid-free
paper and bound in the United States of
America.

Library of Congress Cataloging in Publication Data

Weigel, John A.
    Patrick White.

    (Twayne's world authors series;
TWAS 711. Australian literature)
    Bibliography: p. 135
    Includes index.
    1. White, Patrick, 1912–
—Criticism and interpretation.
I. Title. II. Series.
PR9619.3.W5Z944   1983   823   83-12599
ISBN 0-8057-6558-1

*For Jane LeCompte,
Elizabeth Tobin,
and Jennifer Walker*

Contents

About the Author

John A. Weigel is Professor in English *Emeritus*, Miami University, Oxford, Ohio. With advanced degrees in literature (Case Western Reserve University) and psychology (Columbia University) he has both alternated and crossed fields. He has published many book reviews, professional articles, and verses. He is the author of three other books in the Twayne series: *Lawrence Durrell, Colin Wilson,* and *B. F. Skinner.*

Preface

On October 18, 1973, the Nobel Prize for Literature was awarded to an Australian by the name of Patrick White "for an epic and psychological art which has introduced a new continent into literature." Those who make it their business to exploit such news immediately went to work. That evening reporters and sightseers besieged the "new continent" centered in White's home in Sydney, demanding pictures and interviews or just a glimpse of the suddenly famous man. When White refused to disturb his routine—he had already retired for the night—and meet the reporters knocking on his door, he was informed that he might not get "any international publicity" unless he got up at once.

I, for one, was happy to learn that he kept them all waiting until his usual rising time, six o'clock the next morning. Despite the delay, the international publicity followed willy-nilly. A few of us who had felt that Patrick White's artistry was our secret discovery were bemused as we watched the scramble for information and texts. Most libraries owned one or two copies of White's *The Aunt's Story*, a novel which had been used as an assigned text in literature classes. A few had also purchased *The Tree of Man* when it had been recommended by cautious reviewers for its readability and serious theme. But that was about all they had by Patrick White. Secondary material was even more difficult to find. Pioneers in the "fossicking" (Australian for "picking over") of White's writings had published in obscure places and usually at very modest length. It was not easy to become an instant authority on the new prize winner.

Inevitably what White has called "the academic vultures" moved in. White's writing was measured for its mystical unity and/or disunity, for its mythic universality and/or parochialism, for its Christian and/or Jewish theology, for its Jungian and/or Freudian symbolism, imagery, and metaphors. Quite rightly, scholar-critics discovered ambiguities, ambivalences, and paradoxes. Also, more shamefully, grammarians proved White's illiteracy, citing fragments, dangling modifiers, and fractured syntax. A few enthusiasts tried to demonstrate that White did not mean anything he said, and chauvinists tested him for patriotism and/or treason.

I am grateful for all this activity, for the upgrading of dissertations into books and articles, for the debates and even the acrimony. I acknowledge many indebtednesses to those who have tried to reduce White to pedestrian meaning or to elevate him to saintly transcendence. The insights of others, however, have sometimes suffered from having been articulated too soon. Since 1973 White has rounded off a long career—not necessarily ended it, of course—with two more important novels, a collection of stories, a play, and a book-length "self-portrait."

For me Patrick White is properly measured as a candidate for greatness although his writing is not uniformly successful. I believe he is a visionary with a sense of humor. His wit is often acerbic, and I agree with him that there is much "black in White." I also believe he is really an Australian writer, although the "matey" qualities of Joseph Furphy and Henry Lawson are more obviously indigenous than White's urbane prose. He is an elitist but not an expatriate like Henry Handel Richardson and Miles Franklin. If Australia has occasionally broken his heart, it may be because he has always tried to love it. In any event, he has lived there the greater part of his creative life.

Finally, I confess I was born in the same year (1912) as White. In my *emeritus* status I no longer need to be an "academic vulture." My book is a labor of love: I have all the degrees and credits I shall ever need. It has been exciting and rewarding to study the works of a man who has recently identified himself as "a lapsed Anglican egotist agnostic pantheist occultist existentialist would-be though failed Christian Australian."

I am grateful to the following—arranged in alphabetical order—for their help with this book: Michelle Dunnavant, Joseph Jones, Betty Marak, Rebecca Morgenson, Jill Rubin, Milton White, and William A. Wortman.

John A. Weigel

Miami University

Acknowledgments

The following excerpts are reprinted by permission of Viking Penguin, Inc.

From *The Aunt's Story*. Copyright 1948, © renewed 1976 by Patrick White.
From *The Burnt Ones*. © 1964 by Patrick White.
From *The Cockatoos*. © 1966, 1968, 1974 by Patrick White.
From *The Eye of the Storm*. © 1973 by Patrick White.
From *Flaws in the Glass*. © 1981 by Patrick White.
From *A Fringe of Leaves*. © 1976 by Patrick White.
From *Happy Valley*. Published in 1940 by the Viking Press, Inc. All rights reserved.
From *The Living and the Dead*. Copyright 1941, © renewed 1969 by Patrick White.
From *Riders in the Chariot*. © 1961 by Patrick White.
From *The Solid Mandala*. © 1966 by Patrick White.
From *The Tree of Man*. © 1955 by Patrick White.
From *The Twyborn Affair*. © 1979 by Patrick White.
From *The Vivisector*. © 1970 by Patrick White.
From *Voss*. © 1957 by Patrick White.

The following excerpts are reprinted by permission of Sun Books, Melbourne, Australia:
From *Four Plays*. © 1961, 1962, 1963, 1964 by Patrick White.

Chronology

Jews for *Riders in the Chariot*. Play, *The Season at Sarsaparilla*, is staged.

1963   Play, *A Cheery Soul,* is staged.

1964   First collection of short stories, *The Burnt Ones*. Play, *Night on Bald Mountain*, is staged.

1965   *Four Plays*.

1966   Seventh novel, *The Solid Mandala*.

1970   Eighth novel, *The Vivisector*.

1973   Ninth novel, *The Eye of the Storm*. Receives Nobel Prize for Literature.

1975   Second collection of short stories, *The Cockatoos*.

1976   Tenth novel, *A Fringe of Leaves*.

1977   Play, *Big Toys*, is staged.

1979   Eleventh novel, *The Twyborn Affair*.

1981   *Flaws in the Glass: A Self-portrait*.

Chapter One
Patrick White: *Flaws in the Glass*

In his seventieth year Patrick White has published what he calls a "self-portrait" to distinguish it from a definitive auto-biography or intimate memoir. *Flaws in the Glass*[1] is never-theless fully three-dimensional. It is frank and specific about the writer's family, friends, and lovers as well as the major influences upon his writing. In it White emphasizes his strug-gle to identify himself during his childhood and adolescence. Wealthy turn-of-the-century Australian families such as the Whites still looked to Europe and particularly to England for their cultural roots. At the same time they were often defen-sive about their colonial status. White's personal search for identity was complicated by his birth in England, his homo-sexuality, and his literary precociousness.

Early Years

Patrick White was born in England on May 28, 1912. Dick and Ruth White, an affluent Australian couple, had been traveling abroad and stopped in London for the birth of their first child. In his self-portrait White is candid about his views toward his parents. He remembers his mother as "the titular mother" (15); he confesses that although at times he respected her, he never really loved her; he notes her vanity, her ambitions, and her pretensions. White concedes that she was a model for the imperious old lady in his novel *The Eye of the Storm*. White's father was a member of a respected family whose commercial success had assured their social status without impugning their honor. Dick White did not understand his son, and White confesses that he never knew

1

his father well, even when as a lonely child he might have
been tempted to move closer to his father. White sums him
up as "an Australian chauvinist of the old order" (129).

Lacking rapport with his parents and at odds most of the
time with his younger sister, the boy turned to others for af-
fection and understanding. Lizzie Clark, for example, who
joined the household as a nanny when Patrick's sister Sue
was born, became a surrogate mother. He also made friends
with a black servant and eventually with a few unconven-
tional and more distant members of the White family.

Although Patrick was returned to Sydney when he was six
months old, presumably to continue the White dynasty
as a fourth-generation Australian descended from English
yeomen, his family intended to make him as British as possible. His education followed the pattern designed for the sons
of Australian gentlemen. He dutifully attended two lower
level schools at home, Cranbrook in Sydney and Tudor
House in Moss Vale, the latter a boarding school, to initiate
him into the ways of the British public school. He was then
sent to England where he attended Cheltenham College near
Gloucester.

Young Patrick experienced the ambiguity of his personal
heritage one day at Tudor House when Dame Melba, the
famous Australian soprano, visited his class. When she asked
the students born in Australia to raise their hands, Patrick
was the only one in the room with his hand down. After he
admitted that he had been born in London, Dame Melba
"muttered with the glowing glint of the professional expatriate, 'Not a bad place *either*'" (19). Although she had
lessened his shame, he knew that he had alienated his Australian-born classmates. Later White would appreciate that his
heritage posed a dilemma he would never quite solve and
that his mother's obsession with her son's education was
part of an inescapable historical situation. Though born in
England, Patrick shared the uneasiness of most Anglo-Saxon
Australians about their identities.

There were other differences that precluded White from
advancing into easy "mateship" with boys. In the Australian
tradition a mate is another male you can count on as your
best friend. A mate is clearly distinguishable, however, from

a lover. Schoolboys traditionally tolerate mild romances between one another but an adult is not supposed to love a man with the same intensity he loves a woman—nor, of course, to express that love erotically. Australian mateship fills the gap between heterosexual and homosexual love; however, Patrick White, unlike his friends, experienced no such gap.

White asserts that even when he was very young he did not worry about evidences of his "sexual ambivalence" (34). He remembers having his first erection when he was seven years old, and he calmly admits that he "indulged" early and frequently. His Australian boarding school officially banned all sex with the result that sex was very much talked about and experimented with outside the classrooms. "Sex was," White writes, "the theme developed in the dormitories, in the tunnels of drought-stricken laurels, and the long grass hedged in by hawthorn" (27). What he calls "boyish orgasms" and the "agonies of sexual jealousy" became for him important extracurricular activities. He felt little guilt: "I can still experience my schooldays in the country as a synthesis of living sensuality," he writes, citing as examples "bread and mushrooms frying in biscuit tins on a schoolroom stove, hot darkness and spilt semen" (27).

There were also some unequivocally good moments during his schooldays in England, including a few friendships and a stimulating summer holiday at Dieppe, which he describes as "a brief flirtation with France and the French language" (36). The result of his learning French was his ability finally to "unlock" Gustave Flaubert's *Madame Bovary*, a novel which became for him, as it has for many writers, the epitome of fastidious prose. He was also developing a taste for serious music, undergoing a "crash course" in the operas of Massenet. He began to study the plays of Chekov, Ibsen, and Strindberg, and to attend the theater in London. He and a friend, Ronald Waterall, "spent hours hanging around stage doors waiting for the stars to come out" (54). He was not particularly disappointed when they seemed less ethereal close-up than they had on the stage, for he was beginning to accept the fact that there was more than one fascinating level of reality.

Young Manhood

Instead of going directly to Cambridge University after graduating from Cheltenham College, White returned home. The decision was his first break with his mother's schedule. He had been increasingly eager for the freedom which he expected to follow his leaving school. Back in Australia, however, he soon discovered that he had become a stranger in his own country. "I had been released from prison of course," he remembers, "but freedom was not what I expected. . . . My gaol sentence had left its stamp; I met with suspicion and often undisguised dislike" (46).

The irony of his situation was becoming clearer and clearer. During his four years at school in England he had been under suspicion as an Australian. Now back home his English inhibitions and accent began to alienate him from the few friends he had made there as a boy. He was particularly hurt when the man who trained his father's horses began to treat him as a "real gentleman" (47). Also, he was lonely and "badly wanted to love someone" (47). The eligible girls his mother arranged for him to meet were not his intellectual equals and did not interest him sexually. White confesses that his "chemistry lacked some essential property" (48).

Adding to his alienation was his growing conviction that he wanted to be a writer. His parents did not approve of his leanings: "An artist in the family tree was almost like a sodomite; if you had one you kept him in the dark" (57). It would not be long before his mother would refer to him as a "freak" and he had already heard himself called a "changeling."[2] Although he was aware that his differences from others would be apparent, he says that he was not prepared for "the shock of returning to Australia" (47).

What did finally keep him alive and sentient in Australia was what he calls "the landscape." The therapeutic aspect of nature in White's life is reflected in his work. He did not, however, at that time—nor ever—hear the "still, sad music of humanity" that Wordsworth listened to in nature after his "hour of thoughtless youth" had passed. White prefers his landscapes to remain silent and devoid of human beings. "The ideal Australia I visualized," he writes in retrospect, "during any exile and which drew me back, was always

. . . a landscape without figures" (49).

White and his family agreed on a compromise. Instead of returning to England and Cambridge he was to try working as a jackeroo, which is the Australian equivalent of a cowboy. For two years he more or less successfully simulated a jackeroo. He remembers, however, bathing with his fellow workers "without quite becoming their equal" (51). Furthermore, he was spending most of his evenings "writing by lamplight" instead of pursuing girls. White insists that these "early effusions by lamplight . . . were more honest in their lumbering after truth" than his "subsequent chase after a fashionable style in London . . ." (52). He has also exalted his "frustrated longings for sexual fulfillment" during his jackeroo interlude as "more deserving of reward than the conscious traps I began setting for love, and which usually went off at half cock" (52).

After a two-year intermission White returned to England and entered Cambridge, feeling renewed: "I was experiencing the transport of sinking my roots in richer soil" (38). Although he had passed the entrance examinations in History, he decided on his arrival to "read" French and German instead. He knew that he did not have "a scholar's mind." He was, nevertheless, hungry for knowledge and experience that "might at some future date be put to some practical, aesthetic, or even poetic use" (38). He refers modestly to his "rag-bag of a disorderly mind." "For them [academic critics] the controlled monochrome of reason, for me the omnium gatherum [*sic*] of instinctual colour which illuminates the more often than not irrational behaviour of sensual man" (38).

Prewar Years

When White received the B.A. degree from Cambridge in 1935, he was faced with the need to make a critical decision. In his love-hate affair with Australia, his homeland always appealed to him more and more the longer he stayed away from it. His memory of Australia had again been simplified to "the landscape." But London could not be as easily abstracted or turned into a symbol. It was too close and too alive for the young man to resist. In London he would be nearly anonymous—a heady kind of freedom—while in Sydney he feared that he would be spotted as a failure by his family and "the society to which we belonged" (57). He decided not to go home.

Upon first arriving in London, White rented a "bedsitter" in a house in Ebury Street. Although an allowance from his father soon enabled him to move into a small flat of his own across the street, his first lodging house and its landlady, a Swiss widow, were to become pedal points in White's later fugues from reality. The landlady, Inez Imhoff, resembled his old nanny, Lizzie, "with Italian temper replacing Scottish discretion" (56). She would appear later only slightly altered as a character in his play, *The Ham Funeral*.

Settled in London, White began to write earnestly. He also began to meet stimulating and creative people, some of whom shared his sexual ambivalence but apparently did not feel his kind of anxiety. He discovered that it was not always necessary for him to wear a mask. He particularly credits one new friend he made early in his London adventure with helping to advance his education and to support his literary ambitions. Roy de Maistre, a successful painter related by marriage to White's godmother, had been known by name only to young White. When White called on de Maistre in London he found a charming and informed man twenty years his senior. Of his feelings White says quite simply: "I fell in love very quickly" (59).

The sexual relationship which White had hoped for, however, was wisely modified by the older man into a friendship as de Maistre became White's "intellectual and aesthetic mentor" (60). In his friend's salon White met artists and writers whose unorthodoxy he began to understand. He particularly remembers Francis Bacon, with "his beautiful pansy-shaped face, sometimes with too much lipstick on it" (62). Soon Bacon's disregard of conventional morality—he lived with an old nanny who shoplifted for him and an alderman who was his lover—fascinated the young White. He gradually realized that he, too, had a right to his own personal style.

During these prewar years in London, White says he learned "to walk in the present instead of lying curled . . . in that over-upholstered cocoon, the past, refuge of so many Australians then and now'' (60). He remembers ''paying lip-service to the fashionable radical views'' but he admits that he was ''not interested in politics'' (63). The serious events in Spain and Germany were too remote. Furthermore, he was too insecure to commit himself. Still in his mid-twenties, he often saw himself as a ''mouse-coloured non-personality'' (63). He was, however, a hungry mouse, as he knew: ''But in the days before the Second World War the mouse only haunted, grateful for the crumbs of mere recognition, while wanting desperately to belong to something, to devour somebody passionately'' (63). The war years that followed first intensified his loneliness and then fortuitously resolved it once and for all.

War Years

White was in the United States when England declared war in 1939. He had just sold his first novel, *Happy Valley*, to the Viking Press, and was working on *The Living and the Dead*. Optimistic for the first time about his career as a writer, he was detached from the war and its potential threat to the civilization he had taken for granted in England and on the Continent. He was alerted, however, to the possible effect of war on his career. He says he visualized his ''literary hopes [being] carried away by the flood of history'' (74).

White decided, after a few days of hesitation, to return to England instead of Australia. However, he soon found wartime London depressing. This was, White remembers, ''the music-hall phase of the war when we were hanging out our washing on the Siegfried line. We never stopped complaining. We went to the same restaurants if we could afford them, and gorged ourselves on luxuries. We went to the theatre as we always had. We rustled up rather more intimate parties, and had adventures in the blackout'' (76).

To escape ''this cynical, uneventful, dispiriting phase of life'' (77), White again traveled to New York, but after an abortive relationship with a Park Avenue physician, he returned to London, where he had to wait only a short time before he was drafted. Because of his literacy, defined as his knowledge of two foreign languages, he was made an Intelligence Officer in the Royal Air Force and posted to the Middle East.

White was bemused when his uniform instantly changed his outward appearance. He was, of course, now considered to be doing the right thing. He was too honest with himself, however, to experience a significant internal change, at least not for some months. "I was embarrassed," he writes, "knowing that inside the uniform I was still myself" (84). He hated to salute other officers and so avoided meeting them whenever he could. To the professional officers White was merely an amateur, and indeed he was content to remain an amateur throughout the war.

All in all, White says that he was more bored than frightened by the war, even when he was occasionally exposed to personal danger from bombs or snipers' bullets. The only wound he suffered was a strained ligament in his ankle as the result of stumbling into a trench during an attack early in his Egyptian assignment. The accident was a legitimate excuse for a leave, which took him to Alexandria and a chance meeting with a Greek named Manoly Lascaris—the friend who was to give "direction and meaning to what up till now had been a pointless and often desperate existence" (100). White was introduced to the personable Lascaris by a doubtful baron, an eccentric who hosted a salon frequented mostly by "flibbertigibbets and sycophants" (99). Lascaris, however, White learned later, was far from being either.

Manoly Lascaris was born in Cairo, August 5, 1912. Like White, he never related significantly to either of his parents. Lascaris's father was a Greek from Smyrna. His mother, White writes, was "a Roman Catholic from Vermont, in her background Mayhew of London, President Coolidge, and Aunt Bessie Rorke who sang in the Chicago Opera chorus" (101). The mother abandoned her husband and six children when Manoly was six years old, and the father left home soon after that. The children were eventually turned over to servants, governesses, and relatives in Athens, where the fortunes of the family declined during the occupation of Greece.

Shortly after White and Lascaris met, the latter was drafted into the Greek army being assembled in the Middle East. Like White, Lascaris remained an amateur soldier, even after his fluent English got him a job as an interpreter. Eventually commissioned on the basis of his literacy, he was never completely accepted by his colleagues. For one thing, he seemed too English not to be distrusted by the Greeks, and he was still too Greek to be an authentic Englishman. His situation resembled White's, whose British accent offended Australians while his colonial status was equally offensive to Englishmen. Both men were outsiders, and as the bond between them strengthened during the war years, when they could meet only infrequently and as secretly as possible, they decided to have a go at a permanent relationship—a seldom-successful arrangement between homosexuals. White frankly credits Lascaris with keeping them together the past forty years as he refers to his friend affectionately as "this small Greek of immense moral strength" (100).

After a year stationed in Haifa in what was then called Palestine, White spent the final year of the war in Athens, where he got to know Lascaris's family and cultural heritage. He also fell in love with Greece. His memory of the Parthenon, for example, mixes sweet and bitter emotions. "Rising above the city," he writes, "the Parthenon had not yet begun to look like an archaeological artefact; it suggested pure spirit for this last moment in time before human cattle from the four corners of the earth began to shake its foundations as they trample in herds over the Acropolis" (116). His pleasure in the Acropolis was like his love of landscape: the emptier of human figures the better. Except for a guard, he was often the only person visiting the ruins. Under such circumstances it was easier to see "the Parthenon as the symbol of everything I or any other solitary artist aspired to before we were brought down into the sewage and plastic of the late Twentieth Century" (116). As a postscript to his peroration White adds: "Don't despair however, any of you who have continued reading; it is possible to recycle shit. Could this be my positive message to the Australian optimistic jingle-writers of today?" (116).

Back to Australian Reality

At the end of the war White was tempted to stay in Greece despite the fact that he realized expatriates were "never much more than a joke" (123). When Lascaris offered to mi-

grate to Australia, White decided to go home, and he began
"preparing . . . to face an Australian reality which Manoly
could not have begun to understand" (123). He knew that
when Lascaris joined him the two would have to disguise
their relationship. Furthermore, being a writer was not quite
respectable in Sydney. "Writers still lived concealed like
borer in the trunk of a shrub . . ." (135). His disaffection was
lessened only by his excitement over the unexpectedly viable "art world" he found in Sydney, of which the most
prominent representative was William Dobell, a painter
whose work eventually influenced White's writing although
later White felt that Dobell became too commercial.

During these days of uncertainty and depression, waiting
in Sydney for Lascaris and feeling ambivalent about his
hopes for a lasting relationship, he was working on what became his third novel, *The Aunt's Story*. When Lascaris arrived, he and White began housekeeping in an old house at
Castle Hill near Sydney. They had bought the house and the
surrounding six acres partly for the pigsties that could be
converted into kennels for their four schnauzers. Because
the place had been called a farm by the previous owners, the
two men obligingly became farmers, keeping two cows and
trying to cultivate the land. The neighbors were amused
while "waiting," White writes, "for us to be driven out.
. . . We lasted eighteen years," he boasts, "not as farmers ad-
mittedly, but as stubborn human beings" (138).

In many ways, White admits, he hated those eighteen
years at Castle Hill. For one thing the house was "almost
waist-deep in weeds" and he was often ill with asthma. With
the help of his partner, however, he "grappled" with his fre-
quent bouts of illness just as he did with "the resistant novels
I had inside me" (139). He began to work on his fourth
novel, *The Tree of Man*, at the kitchen table when his illness
precluded his lying down. When *The Aunt's Story* was
published in 1948, it was hailed tepidly, even hostilely by
Australian critics. Or at least White felt so, and his disappointment added to his illness and depression. At the time he
felt that the purpose of his life was threatened. He considered giving up writing altogether. Only the presence of
Lascaris sustained him, the friend he "had brought on a wild

goosechase to the other side of the world" (144).

A decisive turning point in his mood came one rainy night when, while feeding the dogs, he slipped and fell on his back. With the rain pelting down on him he furiously cursed the God in whom he did not believe. Realizing almost at once the implications of his blasphemy, which of course had assumed the existence of the Deity whom he was cursing, he started to laugh at his "helplessness and hopelessness. . . . My disbelief," he remembers, "appeared as farcical as my fall. At that moment I was truly humbled" (144).

White and Lascaris began "an exercise in organized humility" after his "fall." They attended a few Church of England services at Castle Hill but stopped going when the rector "declared it sinful to guess the number of beans in a jar at the annual church fete" (145). They also sampled the more formal services at Christchurch St. Lawrence in Sydney. Although they found the services "unintelligible" they did enjoy "some nice moments of theatre as the acolytes, including a young Chinese, strolled among the faithful weaving veils of incense" (145).

Seven years elapsed between the publication of *The Aunt's Story* in 1948 and *The Tree of Man* in 1955. The relatively favorable critical reception of *The Tree of Man* was reassuring, and White went back to writing steadily. His fifth novel, *Voss*, was published in 1957. In the same year *The Tree of Man* was awarded the Australian Literary Society Gold Medal, and in 1958 *Voss* was also recognized as serious literature when White received the Miles Franklin Award for it. In 1962 he received the same award for his sixth novel, *Riders in the Chariot*. These awards were locally prestigious; nevertheless, White's possible greatness remained moot. His work was often considered pornographic if not unintelligible. Against some opposition, four of his plays were produced in the early 1960s. White was busy but not yet acclaimed.

After eighteen years at "Dogwoods," their little farm at Castle Hill, White and Lascaris moved into the city, to a comfortable house at 20 Martin Road, in a "good" section of Sydney called Centennial Park. The "great upheaval," as White remembers it, occurred October 13, 1963. Castle Hill had become too suburban. Also, the two men realized that their cultural needs would be more easily met if they lived nearer to the theaters and other attractions in Sydney. At first, however, White had been afraid of the move, "afraid to sever the spiritual roots I had put down in that originally uncongenial soil" (146).

White's roots, however, once more survived transplanting. *The Solid Mandala* was published in 1966 followed by the two novels he says "belong to Sydney," namely, *The Vivisector* (1970) and *The Eye of the Storm* (1973). By that time White had to be taken seriously. Despite his rejection of orthodox Christianity, he was awarded the Nobel Prize for Literature in 1973. The austere judges had found his major works compatible with Alfred Nobel's stated intention that the literary prize should honor only writers with an "idealist tendency." The publication of *The Eye of the Storm* just previous to the decision by the committee allegedly helped counteract the cynical tone of *The Vivisector*, which is far from a comfortable novel to read if the reader is questing after spiritual consolation. The official citation announced that Patrick White was honored "for an epic and psychological narrative art which has introduced a new continent into literature."

Although Lascaris feared at the time that their "lives would never be the same" (250), White's lifestyle did not change very much. He refused to go to Sweden, sent a friend instead to receive the award, and subsequently gave the money away. Some years before, when he and Lascaris moved into the city, they had tried socializing. They found it not to their taste, White objecting to the hypocrisies of "rank and riches" as well as discovering that all too often he was famous for the wrong reasons. The Nobel Prize added notoriety to his literary fame as the press and curiosity seekers began to besiege his home. When what he calls "the academic vultures" began to invade his privacy, he refused to be interviewed or otherwise interrupt his work and personal life. White has managed to survive the success that came to him suddenly—too suddenly, perhaps, for it to seem real to him or to some of his admirers who had never predicted that his best writing could become popular in the worst sense of that word.

In 1958 White had written that he "was determined to prove the Australian novel is not necessarily the dreary, dun-coloured off-spring of journalistic realism."[3] Twenty-five years later he has every right to feel that he has succeeded in reaching his goal. In the decade since receiving the Nobel Prize he has published two major novels, *A Fringe of Leaves* (1976) and *The Twyborn Affair* (1979), neither of which could possibly be called "dreary" or "dun-coloured." He has also continued his interest in the theater, adapting his short story, "The Night the Prowler," for the cinema in 1977, and producing a socially conscious play, *Big Toys*, the same year.[4] His recent self-portrait, modestly called *Flaws in the Glass* (1981), admits that his "pursuit" of "razor-blade truth" has made him "a slasher." In conclusion, however, he quickly qualifies his touch of cynicism: "Not that I don't love and venerate in several senses—before all, pureness of heart and trustfulness" (155).

Chapter Two

The Search for an Idiom: From *Thirteen Poems* to *The Living and the Dead*

Patrick White has never concealed his literary sophistication nor his impatience with provincialism. Like his distinguished Australian-born predecessor, Henry Handel Richardson, White has known and drawn upon a rich European tradition. He was educated in England, read French and German at Cambridge, and has always been an enthusiastic traveler and polylinguist. Unlike Richardson, however, who spent most of her life outside her native land, returning only once for a six-weeks visit after leaving there at the age of seventeen, White has made Australia his home since 1948. Although an expatriate, Richardson exploited memories of her childhood and the experiences of her father in her trilogy, *The Fortunes of Richard Mahony* (1930), which is accepted as a great Australian novel because it is authentic in details. White, too, except in his second novel, *The Living and the Dead*, and in some of his short stories, has used Australian settings, characters, and events in his fiction. Unlike Richardson's novels, however, White's fiction had to struggle for recognition in Australia.[1]

The difference is in the timing. Richardson was born in 1870, White in 1912. *The Aunt's Story*, White's first successful novel, was published more than a year after Richardson's death. Writers of Richardson's generation were divided into two groups: the more or less illiterate regionalists, like Joseph Furphy [Tom Collins] and Henry Lawson, who loved Australia as they knew it and wrote affectionately about swagmen, bushmen, and squatters; and the literate elitists, like Richardson. The latter were expected to compete with English writers and, like other privileged fellow citizens who were educated abroad, were allowed to speak and write English rather than Australian. Most literate writers of Richardson's generation admired Henry James and aspired to his urbanity no matter what subjects they might choose for their fiction.

When Henry James died in 1916, several literary giants were beginning to challenge his supremacy. James Joyce, D. H. Lawrence, Virginia Woolf, and T. S. Eliot, who were all born in the 1880s, rejected traditional chauvinisms in both style and ideas. Their experiments in prose and poetry opened new vistas, enlarged the scope and importance of fiction and poetry, and reached for universals. As they aimed at nothing less than greatness they inspired many younger writers.

Patrick White, too, strove to write significant literature rather than merely to please the provinces. Even as a child he had dashed off a tragedy in blank verse, using Shakespeare as his model. Later he was much influenced by the new giants, who themselves had not feared discontinuities in their prose and poetry, had introduced symbols and images as valid and basic units of communication, and had rejected traditional grammar and syntax as academic. Eliot's *The Wasteland* (1922), for example, made images of decay and chaos beautiful and meaningful. To make sense in the old ways of logic and congruity was no longer to make sense. Sense and sensibility were interchangeable, and only dullards needed to understand prose or poetry.

White had also gone to school to earlier experimentalists. As a child he had read voraciously and indiscriminately, discovering good and bad writers and trying to unlock the secrets of the former while discarding the tricks of the latter. He studied the works of Flaubert, Chekov, Ibsen, and Strindberg as "good" writing. He read the Bible and investigated other soothsayers, such as Jung and Freud. He measured the alleged greatness of Goethe and found he preferred Tolstoy as "the only literary genius who survives his own hypocrisy."[2] He also concluded, perhaps rather hastily, that his Australian predecessors had little to teach him.

Early Poems and Plays

White's first publication was a slim and undated volume of verses modestly titled *Thirteen Poems*, privately printed, unsigned but initialed "P. V. M." for the author's first three names. The contents represent work written before 1930.[3] Not unexpectedly, these little poems do not predict the writer's later success, and fairly enough are negligible, for they were meant to be seen only by family and friends. One of them begins: "Squalor / All is squalor / Everywhere the stench of cabbages / And overflowing garbage tins." T. S. Eliot might have approved but he also would not have feared serious competition from young Patrick White.

White persisted in trying to write poetry until he discovered that prose fiction could also be lyrical and a stronger vehicle for projecting his imagination. In the interim, however, he published another slim volume of verse, *The Ploughman and Other Poems*. Dated 1935 and limited to three hundred copies, this volume, like *Thirteen Poems*, is quite rare.[4] A product of White's Cambridge years, the collection represents his last serious attempt to adapt verse to his artistic purposes. There is nothing compelling about either technique or imagery in this early writing. In the title poem, for example, the poet describes his hero as "Ploughing, ploughing, ploughing the bones of the centuries into the earth." If the "bones of the centuries" are too abstract to see or feel, the poem is redeemed at the end when the plowed field is "strewn with gulls."[5] Incidentally, White's gulls and other birds keep flying throughout his novels.[6]

White's tentative phase also includes serious attempts to write for the stage. He had been stagestruck since he first discovered the live London theater during his undergraduate days at Cheltenham College in England. Between 1933 and 1939 White valiantly kept on experimenting with the dramatic idiom. Although none of his early plays has been published or has survived in manuscript—White himself is indifferent to their fate—something is known about them. One three-act comedy and one one-act comedy were performed at Bryant's Playhouse in Sydney between 1933 and 1935. Also, White apparently wrote sketches and lyrics for revues produced in 1935 at London's Little and Gate

Theatres.[7] He had also finished a more ambitious play, *Return to Abyssinia*, before World War II. It was, however, not produced until 1947 at Bolton's Theatre in London, when it was reviewed in the *Times* (London) as "a disarmingly ingenuous little play."[8]

Early Fiction

Among White's early publications are two short stories which more clearly than his other early writing point forward toward his mature work although they are still overburdened with indebtedness to his predecessors. In "The Twitching Colonel," which appeared in the prestigious *London Mercury* in 1937, White fondles words, confounds points of view, and fractures syntax while recklessly mixing images and abstractions.[9] Virginia Woolf is never far away. Indeed, her novel *The Years* is reviewed in the same issue of the magazine, which also includes pieces by H. G. Wells and Sean O'Faolain and a review of George Orwell's *The Road to Wigan Pier*. White had begun to keep good company.

White's Colonel is a retired army officer with a compulsive twitch and a need for whiskey, both acquired during his years of service in India along with many memories. He has seen the rope trick and has not yet solved it. He is still experiencing the tension between empirical reality and illusion. In short, he is unsure about his own identity and the meaning of life. He is, of course, heckled by children in the neighborhood and only tolerated by his landlady. He is breaking up:

Only in dissolution is salvation from illusion, in dream perhaps that is shadow of death, or decomposition of substance, the frail symbol of reality which man clutches, holding himself by the throat, strangling himself through fear while denying suicide, this is man, this is also Maya, this imperfection that is man denying his shadow as day lengthens, as mind is restless with striving yet afraid of sleep. (607)

The prose flows on and on as the Colonel cracks. He is last seen in a quasi-real, quasi-symbolic fire, dancing on the roof of his rooming house—"climbing rope or smoke and the flame smiles with the warmth of smiles that welcome, no

longer the half-guessed significance of smiles, of wave, or
rope, of the brown eye of jewelled elephants, as slipping ef-
fortless and without elegy the world dissolves . . ." (609).
That is the end of the Colonel, but the author, perhaps uncertain about his success, in the last few lines tells the reader
how to feel about the event: "He is gone, he has disappeared, the poor gentleman, the Twitching Colonel. We are
afraid. We go into our houses. We close our doors. The fire
is exhausted. We creep away. It is something we do not
understand. We are afraid" (609).

A second short story, "Cocotte," which appeared in 1940
in Cyril Connelly's *Horizon*, another prestigious periodical,
is more like a sketch. This time the concern is focused on an
old woman who is apparently confused about reality as she
projects her own needs upon her dog, Cocotte. In a mono-
logue mixing French phrases with flawed English, the
woman addresses a man whom her dog is possibly annoying.
She confides in the stranger that her husband has been gone
for four days, but she says she is "not triste alone in St.
Grégoire. Mais enfin, on s'amuse."[10] She is, of course, rationalizing her loneliness.

Even White's later and more technically sophisticated
short stories—discussed below in context—have remained
controversial; some critics prefer to classify many of them as
novellas and thus avoid faulting them as imperfect short
stories. More to the point, however, is the fact that in his
early pieces of short fiction White was discovering limitations in the genre which he would not have to deal with in
the more spacious novel. Neither of his two earliest short
stories adequately melds substance and image with his
vision.

Happy Valley

Although White long ago rejected *Happy Valley* as his
"best forgotten novel," he was eager enough at first to get it
published in England in 1939 and in the United States in
1940.[11] Its generally positive critical reception pleased him
at the time and certainly encouraged his decision to continue
to write. In fact, it is far from the self-indulgent fictionalized
autobiography typical of many first novels. It is an ambitious

work, carefully planned to support a thesis summarized in the epigraph from Mahatma Gandhi: "It is impossible to do away with the law of suffering, which is the one indispensable condition of our being. Progress is to be measured by the amount of suffering undergone . . . the purer the suffering, the greater is the progress." In order to pack the story with suffering, White created a large cast of characters, distributing among them many problems, ranging from lust to abstinence, from wealth to poverty, and from adolescence to late maturity.

In the tradition of our-town plots, in which unity is forced on diversity by geographical limitations, the action is largely confined to a small valley town near enough to Sydney to be relatively urbane without becoming suburban. The characters, burdened as they are with a thesis to prove, all too often fall to stereotypes as the action rises to melodrama. While the seasons of one year come and go, the author tries one style after another in his eagerness to make the reader see and feel and understand.

Except for the insertion of the adjective "fragile," the opening sentences could have been written by Ernest Hemingway: "It had stopped snowing. There was a mesh of cloud over the fragile blue that sometimes follows snow. The air was very cold." The next sentence, however, introduces the first symbol: "In it a hawk lay, listless against the moving cloud, magnetized no doubt by some intention still to be revealed." And then, as if he realized he had gone too far, the novelist qualifies his image: "But that is beside the point." The reader is informed immediately that the hawk just happened "to be in the sky in a necessary spot at a necessary moment, that is, at nine o'clock in the morning about twenty miles to the south of Moorang . . ." (11).

At that precise time Dr. Oliver Halliday has delivered the publican's stillborn child. On the way home the thirty-four-year-old physician is naturally quite thoughtful. In 1918 he had been sixteen years old and although he still felt that young at times, he had acquired many responsibilities over the years. As the hawk continues to circle overhead, Halliday goes home to his wife Hilda and two young sons, all of whom are more or less unhappy. Hilda suffers from the climate and wants to move to sunny Queensland. The older boy, Rodney, a preadolescent, is afflicted with too much sensibility and is persecuted by his schoolmates. Soon the villain is introduced, Clem Hagan, who also sees the hawk overhead and would kill it if he had a gun. Clem has taken a job as the hired hand for the rich Furlow family, whose daughter Sidney soon has an affair with the virile Clem, who in turn seduces Vic Moriarity, the neurotic wife of the self-pitying schoolteacher. Meanwhile, Halliday begins an affair with the spinster piano teacher, Alys Browne.

As the plot thickens, so does the prose. For example, young Rodney begins to wonder about life: "Growing up then was like this. You were ten. . . . Then time began to race down an avenue cold with stars. You wanted to put up your hands" (252–53). The novelist rises to eloquence: "Waiting, waiting for what, Happy Valley waiting in the dark, is the question without answer. There is no collaboration between human curiosity and the attitude of inanimate things, least of all in the dark. . . . So there is no choice but to fall asleep . . ." (256).

At a critical moment Oliver Halliday and Alys decide to elope. They are driving to Moorang when they come upon the schoolteacher's dead body lying near the highway. Dr. Halliday, knowing his duty, turns back with his mistress to transport the body to Happy Valley. There he also finds the corpse of Mrs. Moriarity, "this thing that had been a woman" (269). The doctor's affair with Alys is ended as he resumes his role as a good citizen. Meanwhile, when Clem Hagan is charged with the murder of Mrs. Moriarity, Sidney Furlow sacrifices her honor by testifying that he was with her at the time of the killing. And when Alys discovers she has lost both her lover and her money, in the tradition of White's best heroines she says: "I shall not hurry . . . I shall shape time with what I have already got" (312).

The Hallidays also yield and leave Happy Valley as the syntax again shatters and hope for the future redeems the failures of the past:

Slipping away the ghost gives the live part of the body purged if it were possible to accept this the wind alive on the face on Oliver Halliday on Hilda Halliday his wife on George and Rodney Halliday that are baptized afresh by wind that points down the valley beyond the post the so many miles that are just so many miles into the future that is Rodney and George may I be an explorer Rodney said. . . . (315–16)

The last sentence of the novel opens up the future: "The car furrowed the road, lapsed into distance and the moving rain" (317).

William Walsh, whose knowledge and understanding of White's fiction is authoritative, evaluated White's first novel fairly: "The prose is fluent and breathless, oddly uncertain in its gait, and wholly lacking that self-excavating and rock-moving force so characteristic of White's full powers, even in their mannered phases."[12] Disagreements about White began early. A New York reviewer called *Happy Valley* "the mature, creative work of a comparatively young man."[13] A London reviewer at the same time decided the "book was depressing to a degree almost unbearable. . . ."[14] Geoffrey Dutton, who felt that White had been too severe in rejecting *Happy Valley*, nevertheless noted the "Joycean flavour of the immature style."[15] R. F. Brissenden praised a few "despite" values: "Despite the force with which the feeling of profound alienation is conveyed, the language here is tortuous and fumbling. . . ."[16]

The Living and the Dead (1941)

White's second published novel, *The Living and the Dead*, was also planned to support a thesis. While his first novel extolled the benefits of suffering as promised in an epigraph from Gandhi, the second is more cautious as it adds pleasure to pain as a value to be investigated. An epigraph from the eighteenth-century philosopher, Helvétius, alerts the reader to the difficulty of understanding the uses of both adversity and good fortune. Helvétius theorizes—in French—that after a person has made many errors and invented many absurd systems, he will some day discover "les principes simples, au développement desquels sont attachés l'ordre et le bonheur du monde moral."[17]

The characters in the novel who presumably will help the reader to discover the simple principles that underwrite order and good fortune in the moral world are perforce more complex and more sophisticated than the small-town folks in *Happy Valley*. Although White has rejected his second novel just as he has the first, noting how he hated working on "the wretched book" in prewar London,[18] it is stylistically and philosophically a marked advance toward his own idiom and a valiant attempt to articulate his own anxieties and doubts. The relative values of action versus contemplation, of indulgence versus abstinence, and of success versus failure are debated in the novel. The author appears to have divided himself into the two main characters, a brother and a sister, and to have distributed his major concerns among a large cast of characters, ranging from sterile intellectuals to political activists, as he tests the validity and viability of various commitments.

The Living and the Dead is White's only London novel. The prewar years that he spent abroad—mostly in England— trying to become a writer gave him plenty of chances to get to know the living and the dead who seemed to him to dominate London's cultural life. Comparing his own relative failure at the time with the apparent successes of others, he was often depressed and uncertain. Most of all he was lonely, for his friend Manoly Lascaris had not yet entered his life and his relationships with other men were casual. He was politically uncommitted although he would like to have been able to take stands on the important current issues. In short, he was personally trying to define the difference between life and death.

Not surprisingly, *The Living and the Dead* asks more questions than it answers, but its very inconclusiveness gives it an aura of honesty as the "wretched book" tries to come alive. Although the style still shows the influence of the verbal virtuosities of Joyce and Woolf, the ambiance of the London setting and the attention to details and nuances make it seem more Jamesian than experimental as the dialogue and action reflect Henry James's preoccupation with values and particularly with the conflict between materialism and less crass sensibilities. Despite the probable intention of the novelist to keep the brother and sister characters central to both action and themes, peripheral characters tend to steal scenes as the story unfolds, among them some definitely shoddy people as well as one noble primitive, Julia Fallon, a servant-nursemaid reminiscent of White's old nanny, Lizzie Clark.

After a prologue in the present, the story returns to the early part of the twentieth century and then slowly moves ahead to an epilogue that partially repeats the prologue. Accidents and improbable coincidences control the lives of the characters often enough to make the unpredictable almost a certainty. The effect is unsettling; first on the characters and then on the reader, as the significance of such disorder remains elusive. Nevertheless, there are certain moments in the novel in which the rhetoric insists on trying to make the action and characters credible.

In the prologue, Elyot Standish, a middle-aged and introspective bachelor, author of several volumes of literary criticism and in general a thoroughly civilized man, is returning from Victoria Station. His sister, Eden, has just entrained for Spain, where she intends to defend the freedom her workingman lover has recently died for in support of a strong commitment which Eden did not share. On the way home Elyot sees a drunken pedestrian fall in front of a moving bus and realizes he might save the man's life if he acts quickly. Elyot, however, cannot or simply will not move, and the man is killed when the bus wheels crush him.

Alone at home, eating the bread and the cheese the faithful Julia has set out for him, he broods over the incident as he visualizes the victim's body in the morgue. He associates the drunk's failure to survive with the equally futile efforts of others he has known, especially of his late mother, Catherine Standish, née Kitty Goose, and of the colorless woman, Connie Tiarks, whose love he could never requite, and finally of his sister's late lover, Joe Barnett. The moment introduces the main characters of the novel and spells out the central concern of the novelist:

Somewhere on a slab perhaps they had laid the queasy legs. But the face drifted behind his own, its lips blowing outward on unshaped words, trying to resist the shapelessness. It was this after all that every one of them had tried to do, his mother building her bright room, Eden taking the train into Europe, the Connie Tiarkses and

Joe Barnetts, each with a nervous but convinced contribution towards the business of living. Putting up a structure in the face of shapelessness, building, if not in brick or stone, resistance to annihilation (12–13).

In the long flashback which follows, the metamorphosis of the siblings' mother from the low-born Kitty Goose into Catherine Standish is detailed. Having worked her way up the social ladder to become the village teacher, Kitty ventures above her station to a party where she meets the dashing Captain Willy Standish. Against many odds, Kitty soon becomes the urbane Mrs. Standish and dutifully bears her irresolute husband two children before the marriage collapses. The Standish household, however, is largely sustained by a servant, Julia, who at the age of sixteen "had all the integrity, the dignity, the directness of a Flemish primitive" (57).

As Elyot grows into manhood, he responds coolly to most demands upon his eros and ego. Connie Tiarks, who became almost family when the Standish children were sequestered with her during World War I, patiently woos him, but in vain. No woman will ever completely penetrate his diffidence. He is described as "hateful" and "unreal" by a German girl he rejects: "He aroused emotions he could not return" (142). In contrast to Elyot's withdrawal from sex experience, Eden experiments first with a married man, whose child she eventually aborts without much regret; and then with Julia's relative, Joe. Meanwhile, Connie's unrequited love for Elyot becomes the occasion for a coincidence that ultimately destroys Mrs. Standish, who by this time has preserved enough vitality to accept casual favors from men for casual favors given.

When Connie loses a gift she has addressed to Elyot, it is found by Wally Collins, a brash young saxophonist, who delivers it to the inscribed address and thus by chance meets Mrs. Standish. Soon Mrs. Standish and Wally become ill-matched lovers, an affair in which the aging woman breaks down after attending a tortuous party given by Wally's young and vulgar friends, and dies soon afterwards. Connie is also defeated when Elyot concludes her gift came from a different woman. Even Eden's Joe is defeated. Love is not enough, he discovers, when he remembers that there is "still a sick world mewing at the windowpane, lying with its guts frozen on the sea wall" (296). So he goes off to fight in Spain and is soon killed. In the end, Eden is exhausted but decides to act. After she leaves for Spain, Elyot goes home to eat his bread and cheese: "He felt like someone who had been asleep, and had only just woken" (383).

The equivocal conclusion to the novel confused reviewers. The American publisher announced that "Elyot represented death" while the English publisher identified Elyot with "the possibility of a living future."[19] An American reviewer wrote: "This is a bitter book. Dean Swift's fiercest indictment of humanity was not more painful. . . ."[20] The *Times* (London) compromised: "For all the strain something of poetical apprehension is to be discerned. . . . But egotism flaps too hard and too constantly."[21] William Walsh detected "a talent beginning to assume its true form." Although *The Living and the Dead* has "that basic necessity, a strong constitutive idea . . . the idea does not successfully breathe through and inform every element in the novel."[22]

Chapter Three
The Search for a Subject: *The Ham Funeral* and *The Aunt's Story*

By the end of World War II Patrick White knew that he was committed to being a writer. His early experiments in fiction and poetry had taught him what to reject and what to improve stylistically. He was, however, still tentative about possible subjects. Impatient with the dreary naturalism of many of his contemporaries, he searched himself for ideas compatible with his temperament and found that he had a rich storehouse from which to draw. "I grew drunk," he writes in his autobiography, "cultivating a garden of words and sensations which had been waiting years to germinate."[1]

White's first two postwar works, *The Ham Funeral* and *The Aunt's Story*, show evidences of his verbal intoxication. Characters are made to speak in ways that in real life would indict them as insane or pretentious. Ordinary objects like chairs and tables are elevated to symbols. Some become metaphors for sacraments as the author reaches for epiphanies. Rhetorical questions abound. Chosen characters are given enigmatic qualities as if only the elusive and the equivocal are ultimately true. White's para-grammatical prose alternates between lyricism and the vernacular. Tempering irony with humor and spirituality with lustiness, he manages to keep the audience or reader interested in the story. In a word, he has become professional.

The Ham Funeral (1947)

White's first serious play is unusually precocious for the time it was written. He says he finished it in 1947 although it had been germinating long before that. Although the playwright may have been influenced by Tennessee Williams's innovative drama, *The Glass Menagerie*, which opened in March, 1945, in New York, the experiments of Samuel Beckett and Eugene Ionesco in the theater of the absurd were yet to come. By the time White's play was finally produced in Adelaide in 1961 it seemed, of course, much less original. Such devices as characters who address the audience, sets that defy probability—White has a house speak—and nonsequiturs in dialogue and action had become familiar to sophisticated audiences. *The Ham Funeral*, however, is discussed here in the context of the time it was written rather than as a later production. It is important as an early experiment in which the author explores new subject matter.

From the beginning *The Ham Funeral* breaks with the naturalist tradition. Before the curtain rises, a "Young Man" appears and addresses the audience. The playwright's directions demand much skill of the actor playing the part, for the Young Man's "attitude throughout the play," the author explains, "is a mixture of the intent and the absent, aggressiveness and diffidence." He is to be dressed "in a fashion which could be about 1919." He is also "rather pale." [2]

This pale, tentative character, whose name remains uncertain throughout the drama, announces that he has just "woken." Yawning, he goes on to explain that the time and place of the play are unimportant and that he could have been "born in Birmingham . . . or Brooklyn . . . or Murwillumbah. What *is* important is that, thanks to a succession of meat pies (the gristle-and-gravy, card-board kind) and many cups of pink tea, I am *alive!*" (15). Nevertheless, as the play proceeds, the ambiance more and more resembles Cockney London in general and White's former lodging house in Ebury Street in particular.

After the Young Man warns the audience what they are about to see is "a piece about eels" and that it probably is not their "kind of play," he encourages them to "sit it out, and see whether you can't recognize some of the forms that will squirm before you in this mad, muddy mess of eels" (15). He then identifies himself as a failed poet, one who cannot give them a message. "I know too much," he confesses, and then adds: "That is the poet's tragedy. To know too much, and never enough." He reminds the audience that "plays, of course, are only plays. Even the great play of life" (16). These platitudes, presumably, are not meant to elevate the audience but rather to characterize the Young Man. Throughout the play his tone alternates between scorn and irony. Meanwhile, the audience is encouraged to remain uneasy, for nothing is what it seems, and everything could be something else.

When the curtain rises, the audience is confronted with a two-level set. The upper level is divided into two small bedrooms, and the lower level into a basement kitchen-bedroom and a stairwell. As upper-level action contrasts with lower-level action throughout the play, the two levels become obviously symbolic. The cast is economically confined to three principal characters, four secondary characters, and one young woman who plays both her real—and drab—self and the Young Man's "anima," that is, the feminine half of his personality. The Young Man and the woman, whose prosaic name is Phyllis Pither, occupy upper-level rooms separated by a wall penetrated by a locked door. The landlady and the landlord live downstairs. Spotlighting is specified to alternate attention to one level or another or to one part of either level as the action shifts from basement basics, as it were, to higher-level concerns.

In the first scene the upper floor remains darkened as the audience is invited to meet the landlord and the landlady, Mr. and Mrs. Lusty. The man is "vast," and "dressed from neck to ankle in woolen underclothes" (16). The woman is also "large" and "in the dangerous forties, ripe and bursting" (17). It is clear that the Lustys are literally wedlocked. The husband stares and smokes and grunts while his wife prattles on. Her only pleasure is food: "I like to eat. I like something you can get yer tongue around. A nice piece of fat'am, for instance. . . . Or a little bowl of stewed eels. Or a chop with the kidney on it. Or even a bit of bread and drippin', with the brown underneath" (18).

Eventually she invites the Young Man down for a cup of tea, but not before she and the youth indulge in philosophical musings—he about his failure as a poet, she about the death of her only child. The tea ceremony that follows in the basement is the Young Man's preliminary initiation. He adopts both vulgar and mock-heroic mannerisms as he observes his host and hostess bickering with one another. "Is this a tragedy?" he asks himself, and the audience. "Or is it two fat people in a basement, turning on each other?" The landlord then announces his creed: "Life, at last, is wherever a man appears to be." His clichés are suddenly redeemed, however, when "spreading his hand on the table-top" he adds: "This table is love . . . if you can get to know it . . ." (27).

After making his solemn contribution to the drama, the landlord dies abruptly during the next scene. But first the spotlight shifts back upstairs when the Young Man ascends after tea. He informs the audience that his ascension is symbolic: "So resentment creeps back . . . and back . . . as we mount . . . endlessly . . . ." (30). As expected, he consults his neighbor through the closed door between their rooms. Phyllis Pither is an ordinary young woman who is occasionally transfigured by the Young Man's imagination and need into an ethereal spirit. She appears in the first scene merely as an arm in a long white glove touching her side of the door. Now she appears in full figure and full voice as the two neighbors discuss what the Young Man needs to know as a poet. When the anima-girl points to the basement as the answer, he discovers that the landlord has just died.

The Young Man soon becomes involved in the situation as participant and commentator. When the new widow laments the fact that she had not had time to say good-bye to her husband, the Young Man comforts her while informing the audience that they are not to expect definitive answers in this play: "The truth stops where the words begin" (35). He also agrees to notify the landlord's relatives, who live in a house "with the scabs peelin' off" (38). This mission in turn provides the occasion for a surrealist interlude before the curtain. On the way to the relatives' house the Young Man meets two witch-like women, professional scavengers, whose searches into several rubbish bins climax with their discovery of a dead foetus. The women also eat some old letters and a few plastic pearls. The symbolic significance of the scene is spelled out by the Young Man as, Hamlet-like, he contemplates the foetus: "Who'll ever tell where the flesh begins . . . or ends? The landlord and the dead child are one" (43).

When a house suddenly appears, the Young Man suggests that "this could be their house." The house answers him in "the voice of a cold, old man. 'Could be . . . could be . . .'" (43). At that moment four identical relatives appear in four windows of the house although only one emerges to accompany the Young Man to the funeral. In the next scene, however, the four are seen eating ham and chatting with the landlady in the basement. The relatives accuse the widow of many crimes, including the murder of her husband. "Remember 'ow the blood ran," one asks her, "as you turned the knife in 'is side?" (51). Although the charge is not literally true, the landlady admits that she wanted Will dead because he shamed her. "Will's face," she concludes, "saw more than any mirror. Sometimes 'e looked under the skin" (52). (Knives and mirrors will become familiar objects as well as equivocal symbols in White's later fiction.)

In the final scene the landlady and the Young Man seduce each other after a ritual dance. At the climax he feels an urge to kill Mrs. Lusty, but the moment passes and the Young Man prepares to leave forever. Then, all passion spent, he sees the landlady's face not as it really is but as he has transformed it: ". . . lovely in its way . . . the way of those who've lived, and confessed, and survived their own confession" (73). "*As the door closes the whole of the back wall dissolves*," the playwright has specified at the end, "*so that the* YOUNG MAN *is seen walking into the distance through a luminous night*" (74).

The Birth of the Soul of a Poet

White's several dramas have received less critical attention than his stories and novels. They have only recently been considered important enough for a book-length study,[3] although White's biographers have noted the special place in the writer's canon held by *The Ham Funeral*. When it was finally produced in 1961 White wrote a note for the program in which he acknowledged two sources: William

Dobell's painting, *The Dead Landlord*, together with the painter's explanation of how he found his subject in the death of his own landlord and a subsequent ham funeral; and White's own "self-searching" and experience as a young man in the house in Ebury Street.[4] White also admitted that the play "departed from its origins" and was not "naturalistic." Specifically, he explained the relatives as "an expression of the conscience," and the scavengers' interlude as the result of giving "way to my weakness for music hall."[5]

The meaning of *The Ham Funeral* is not difficult to find. There is little doubt, as J. R. Dyce has noted, that the play was intended to be about "spiritual growth and decay: the birth of the soul of a poet . . ."[6] This general theme, of course, returns again and again in White's later works, with variations on the relationship between decay and growth. Decay as a prerequisite to growth appears as often as decay as a consequence of stunted growth. In *The Ham Funeral* the Young Man is in the positive growth phase as he walks out into the night. He is neither insane nor defeated. But what about the landlady? Thelma Herring perceives her as an unsuccessful creation. Mrs. Lusty, the symbol of the flesh which the Young Man must experience as part of his initiation, should have been "more alluring," Herring feels.[7]

Certainly the landlady is less clearly redeemed than the Young Man. She is abandoned at the end despite the poet's momentary perception of her face as "lovely in its way." He is the only one to benefit fully from the sordid sexual encounter as well as the tea ceremony and funeral feast. In contrast to the play, in White's earlier novel, *The Living and the Dead*, there is little hope for anyone at the end. Elyot boarded a bus that was "bound nowhere in particular." The Young Man in the play, however, exits into a "luminous night" which appears as the back wall of the lodging house dissolves. Something magic has happened. The Young Man looks out and then informs the audience that "night was never stiller or closer, I could put out my hand," he says, "and touch it, like a face . . ." (73-74).

Brian Kiernan does not object to White's characterization of the landlady. He observes that Alma Lusty behaves toward the Young Man "both as a mother and a lover," and he ap-

proves of White's "hearty, vulgar realism" in his presentation of the two Lustys. He argues that the poet's "true
growth, and the play's essential development, lies in his being able finally to reconcile his aspirations to 'possess the infinite' with acceptance of Mrs. Lusty. . . .'" It follows, then,
that it does not really matter what happens to the landlady in
the end. The Young Man has learned from her husband that a
table can be love, and from her that a table is not enough. As
Kiernan has phrased it, he learns "the need for simplicity
and humility."[8]

The Aunt's Story (1948)

The Aunt's Story is still White's favorite novel. It was
closer to being a labor of love than earlier works, and certainly the first of the great novels to combine his stylistic
idiom with his dominant concerns. White has admitted in his
autobiography that the central character, Theodora Goodman, was based on his godmother, Gertrude Morrice, whom
he credits "for her unobtrusive opening of windows in my
often desperate youthful mind."[9] He says that he finished
the important and controversial second part of the novel in
Alexandria on the balcony of Manoly Lascaris's flat. It was a
happy time for the two men, who had decided by then to
live together after the war. Not distracted by the music that
came from a nearby cafe, White says that in fact the "radio
churning out non-stop music" was a help, bringing him
"closer to what was happening in Theodora Goodman's
confused mind. . . ."[10]

The Aunt's Story begins in the middle: "But old Mrs.
Goodman did die at last."[11] The event allows Mrs. Goodman's
spinster daughter, Theodora, who had been stranded in an
isolated and frustrating togetherness with the old lady, to
begin her own life—late as it is. After the brief prologue-like
introductory chapter, the story goes back to Theodora's
childhood and carefully establishes special aspects of her
personality.

It is apparent early in her life that Theodora perceives
more levels of reality than those around her. As a child, she
resolves that she will know everything by the time she grows
up. On her twelfth birthday, for example, when the oak tree

in front of the house is struck by lightning, she does not accept the adults' explanation of the event as an act of God. To her the episode remains "one of the things that happened and which it was still not possible to explain" (32). Another event on the same day is equally significant. A friend of Father's from Father's prospecting days is given his dinner on the veranda rather than in the dining room with the family. Understanding between the man and the girl is immediate: "And suddenly the lightning trembled in Theodora, that she had not felt, the lightning that had struck the oak" (33).

Although the strange man tells Theodora he will return, Theodora knows at once that he will not: "In all that she did not know there was this certainty. She began to feel that knowing this might be the answer to many of the mysteries. And she felt afraid for what was prepared" (38).

As Theodora grows up, she spends a short time with her sister in a finishing school, then returns home to try to behave like other young girls. Her father, however, treats her as an equal, teaches her to shoot a rifle like a man, and instructs her in the deeper significances of ordinary-seeming things. For example, he explains that the name of the family estate, Meroë, means a "dead place, in the black country of Ethiopa" (15). Other artifacts, such as her mother's roses and the hills around the house, come to life for her. The hills "conspired with the name, to darken, or to split deeper open their black rock, or to frown with a fiercer Ethiopian intensity" (12). And the roses fragment into "the roselight of morning" and later in the day "the serious full white roses . . . and the lemon-coloured roses" (13).

Fire also fascinates the young Theodora. Once on a rare occasion when she dances with a young man, she and the man become incandescent. As Theodora's striped skirt "streamed with fire" her partner was transfigured into "molten gold" (68–69). Theodora's fire-dance is short-lived, however, for soon thereafter sister Fanny announces her engagement to the young man: "No gong could have beat louder" (75).

After Father's death, Meroë is sold, and Theodora and Mother move to Sydney to a "house above the bay . . . not a

very distinguished house, thin and red, one of a row" (79).
Not much changes. Mrs. Goodman, however reduced her
circumstances, still likes her tea, which she calls "a most
civilized drink" (81). Fanny, recently married, urges
Theodora to consider the same alteration of her life—but
with a difference, of course. Theodora should find someone
"quiet and steady, not necessarily exciting . . ." (87).

   There is, for example, Mr. Clarkson, her mother's solicitor
and a widower with a house "full of exquisite things" (94).
Theodora likes Clarkson, but at the agricultural show she
takes up the rifle at a booth and shatters all the clay ducks,
one by one. Her companions, including Clarkson, are embarrassed: "It was something mysterious, shameful, and grotesque" (113). Exit Clarkson as a suitor. It is now obvious
that Theodora will never marry, but she comforts herself
with the knowledge that at least she is an "aunt," for Fanny
has had a daughter, Lou, whom Theodora adores.

   One morning Theodora picks up a "very thin and impervi-
ous" knife in the kitchen. Suddenly she sees the knife as a
potential murder instrument, as the solution to her confine-
ment. Although she does not follow up on the impulse to kill
her mother, she introjects the guilt, saying to herself: "I am
guilty of a murder that has not been done. . . . it is the same
thing, blood is only an accompaniment" (117).

   When "on a morning the colour of zinc" (122) Mrs. Goodman dies of natural causes, Theodora reacts slowly. She
decides to report the event to her neighbor, a Mr. Love, for
she realizes that "something decent and sad-sounding"
should be said. Knowing that she cannot say it, she relies on
her neighbor to do the honors. But first she does nothing:
"She clenched her hands. She would possess the situation
alone, entirely, firmly, a few moments longer. She held her
mother in her hand" (123).

"Jardin Exotique"

   The second part of this three-part novel picks up
Theodora's life after her mother's death. The setting is more
or less surrealistic—"the Hotel du Midi," where she has
decided to reside indefinitely after traveling extensively in

Europe. "It is sometimes enjoyable just to sit," she tells the manager when she first arrives.

The manager's response is ominous: "Perhaps . . . but first it is necessary to learn" (130). When he recommends the use of his exotic garden where the ladies often take coffee, Theodora dares hope that she has finally found the "goal of a journey," remembering her earlier disappointment in "the gothic shell of Europe" (133). And in fact she begins to relate to the other guests in the hotel. First she meets the youthful Katina, who says she could kiss Theodora "in the particular way I have for aunts" (137).

Theodora also meets the elderly twins, the Demoiselles Bloch, who warn her that they are Jewish, mention the rumors "that Hitler will make a war" (141). A General Sokolnikov writes her a note, sensing Theodora's sympathy. Before long he perceives her as his dead sister, Ludmilla, and Theodora gladly plays the role. When he asks her if she believes in God, she answers: "I believe in this table" (146).

The friends and the friends of friends, both imaginary and substantial, whom Theodora meets or invents during her stay at the Hotel Midi include Katina's Aunt Smaragada, who lives alone in Athens and "prays for the day when the saints will blaze with gold" (171). Katina also confides in her friend that her mother married her father so as not "to be buried alone" (171); whereupon Theodora fantasizes an incident in which she is entertained by Katina's absent parents. There is also Madame Rapallo, who, she is told, is the mother of the glamorous—but absent—Principessa Dell Isola Grande. Madame Rapallo's other claim to significance is her keepsake, a lovely nautilus shell. Soon, however, Theodora is informed that Rapallo has invented the Principessa. The shell is also too fragile to survive and is shattered in a *contretemps* with the general. Meanwhile Wetherby, a former schoolmaster and now a poet, and his lover, Lieselotte, appear. The latter is described as "a snowdrop, quivering, but green-veined. Depravity had tortured the original wax into lines of purest delicacy" (160). Her paintings, General Sokolnikov assures Theodora, are mad. Theodora answers: "Only chairs and tables . . . are sane" (162).

One night the electric power in the hotel fails. The manager announces: "There shall be lamps and candles" (235). Before long, one of those lamps, thrown by Lieselotte at Wetherby in reproach and anger, starts a great fire in which the hotel is destroyed and in which Wetherby and Mrs. Rapallo both die. "It is a tragedy of which one reads in the papers" (243), Miss Griggs, a survivor, announces while enjoying the disaster to the fullest.

"Holstius"

In the third part of the novel Theodora abruptly appears on a train somewhere in "the middle of America" (249). She is, ostensibly, going home. She has even written her sister that "the time has come at last to return to Abysinnia" (250–51), meaning her home, Meroë, but her sister did not respond positively. Suddenly Theodora decides to detrain.

Setting her hat with its black rose on her head, she leaves the train at the next stop, which is a small town, and experiences the dawn, resting on a doorstep, "her head against a tree" (254). When the woman of the house finds her there in the morning and tells her that "you gotta go *some*where," Theodora replies: "I do not particularly want to go anywhere" (256).

Rejecting offers of help from neighbors along a road that leads upward, Theodora begins to ascend and to dismantle her identity by discarding her train tickets, leaving her hat behind, and refusing to give her name. Nevertheless, she appears inoffensive and gentle to those who offer to help her. She evades all of them, however, and finally finds, at the top of the hill, an empty house, which she enters easily after removing the lock and hasp from the door. There, "in the disintegrating world, light and silence ate into the hard, resisting barriers of reason, hinting at some ultimate moment of clear vision" (269). At this moment the novelist is apparently no longer neutral as he labels Theodora's confusion as possible enlightenment.

The coda, which is both the most beautiful and the most obscure section of the novel, is almost impossible to summarize, for each word is heavily weighted with significance. A man enters the house that Theodora has taken over. He speaks: "Evening . . . It's a steep climb up" (270). He then introduces himself: "My name is Holstius." As he puffs on his pipe, lighting it with a stick, Theodora suggests she has seen him somewhere before. He answers: "Possibly" (270). Theodora is reminded of "the Man who was Given his Dinner, and how at the time she had been infused with a warmth of love that was most thinly separated from expectation of sorrow."

When Holstius asks her if she suspects him, she answers: "I suspect myself" (271).

Holstius then explains that she is "torn in two." And when Theodora asks what she is expected to do, Holstius answers: "I expect you to accept the two irreconcilable halves" (272).

Theodora sits on the floor at Holstius's feet. "You cannot reconcile joy and sorrow," he says. "Or flesh and marble, or illusion and reality, or life and death. For this reason, Theodora Goodman, you must accept. And you have already found that one constantly deludes the other into taking fresh shapes, so that there is sometimes little to choose between the reality of illusion and the illusion of reality. Each of your several lives is evidence of this" (272).

Holstius returns once to warn Theodora that "those who prescribe the reasonable life" will come for her. He predicts—without rancor—that she will submit. "They are" he argues, "admirable people really, though limited." When she agrees, Holstius adds: "If we know better we must keep it under our hats" (278).

Theodora understands. When they come for her, she goes with them, putting on the hat which they have returned to her: "The hat sat straight, but the doubtful rose trembled and glittered, leading a life of its own" (281).

"We Must Keep It Under Our Hats"

Critical responses to *The Aunt's Story* range from hermeneutic solutions to exalted praise and equally exalted rejection. Although White had returned to Australia for his heroine, he had not kept her there more than one-third of the way through the novel, and certainly he exploited exotic and foreign settings and characters, finally leaving Theodora in the middle of America. Australian patriots were reluc-

tant to classify him along with native realists such as Kylie
Tenant and Eleanor Dark. The former, for example, who
was born the same year as White, was writing about "real"
Australians, particularly the deprived and unfortunate. Dark,
meanwhile, was researching her historical novels and pro-
posed to tell no less than the whole truth about Australia.
White was distrusted first of all for his rejection of gutsy
bushmen, swagmen, squatters, aborigines, and Chows in
favor of the educated, literate, and essentially urban characters such as the British Standishes in *The Living and the
Dead* and the affluent although Australian Goodmans in *The
Aunt's Story*; and for his idiosyncratic style, shattered syntax, and obscure allusions. White had not yet allayed the
hostility of contemporary patriots who were trying to come
to terms with a culture in passage from a colony to a nation.
Besides, *The Aunt's Story* was pretentious and obscure.

Each of the three parts of *The Aunt's Story* is prefaced by
an epigraph which seems to insist on obscurity. The first,
from Olive Schreiner, refers to a "human soul" that "reaches
that solitary land of the individual experience, in which no
fellow footfall is ever heard." The second, a brief observation by Henry Miller, defines "The great fragmentation of
maturity" as "asserting our dividedness." The third, again
from Olive Schreiner, is an aphorism: "When your life is
most real, to me you are mad." Somehow it was necessary to
reckon with this trio of hints at the novelist's message.

Forcing one or another kind of unity on the work, however, may distort White's artistic intent.[12] If insanity is the
result of experience that causes the individual to maximize
his dividedness, and if that ultimate state is most real to the
individual although it appears to be insanity to others, then
the message of the novel is solipsistic. If the self knows that it
has been fragmented, it is not yet completely fragmented. If
it is truly "all gone" at the end, then there is no way of iden-
tifying with the psychological derangement *reasonably*.

Under Holstius's guidance Theodora ends up an elitist,
condescending to "admirable" people who are nevertheless
"limited." When Holstius advises her to keep that
knowledge under her hat, he is inviting her—and the
novelist the reader—to join in a conspiracy in which the per-

ceptive and sensitive human being protects himself by returning to privacy, whether that privacy be true insanity or a voluntary silence. Early critics did not take kindly to the elitist tone of the second and third parts of the novel. Later, after they had learned how to read Patrick White's fiction, more patient analysts demonstrated that the novel was truly profound and not as obscure as it seemed at first.

For one thing, the rhetoric of the alleged negativism is itself positive as White persuades the reader to accept the premise that insanity may be the only refuge from the cruel rationality of others. The artist-writer who also practices what he preaches, however, would become mute or unintelligibly schizophrenic. Obviously White is not mute although his shattered syntax may sometimes resemble gibberish to hostile or simple readers. Thus White's first great novel poses all the problems, both explicitly and implicitly, that the later works do.

Predictably, two American critics, Orville Prescott and Diana Trilling, faulted the second part of *The Aunt's Story*, saying that they could not understand "Theodora's motivation."[13] They were, it seems, trying the aunt in a court different from the one White had in mind. What made Theodora do what she did, say what she did, and think what she thought was, of course, only the novelist. *His* motivation was artistic, and he was behaving reasonably enough *as an artist* when he created a character who did not behave reasonably. Another American reviewer wrote that the exotic garden episode was "oblique and elliptic, with a good many pages that resist comprehension."[14] Even Peter Beatson, who has usually been able to fit the pieces of a White novel together in such a way that he is satisfied that White believes in the same God that he does, found the middle movement of the novel difficult, wondering whether the events really occur or are "no more than creations of Theodora's ebullient but untrustworthy mind."[15]

If Theodora is indeed untrustworthy, it is possible, nevertheless, to trust the author to tell just how she cannot be trusted so that in the end the reader can rely on her unreliability. To admirers of White's artistry, the case of Theodora's untrustworthiness is not to be tried outside the book. For such partisans, she is a transcendent character in the context of the novel, one who need not answer to common sense and all its drab rationalizations. She is, in a word, super-sane—inside the novel.

It is possible that those who know all this must keep their knowledge under their hats, for such knowledge can be dangerous. Sanity is moot, as Theodora came to realize, and it is simply more convenient to go with "the admirable people" when they come than to insist on having insights that they cannot understand.

Brian Kiernan, somewhat reluctantly, has concluded that *The Aunt's Story* ends in solipsism: "We see through the eyes of a woman who is withdrawing into what the world sees as madness," Kiernan argues, "but as we see the world through her eyes we cannot judge her vision; we can only accept it or reject the novel."[16] Kiernan has identified the kind of crisis a conscientious reader often experiences in trying to assess one of White's messages. The reader resists at first, unwilling to accept the reasonableness of so much irrationality. Later, persuaded by the rhetoric and its razzle-dazzle, he suspends his own reservations. In the end he may even credit White with visionary powers. The experience becomes more and more pertinent in the later novels, stories, and plays as Patrick White projects his chosen subjects in his own way.

Chapter Four
The Search for
a Commitment: *The Tree of Man* and *Voss*

By the time he completed *The Aunt's Story* Patrick White had found an idiom and a subject that pleased him. He has always liked that novel and has never conceded that it is either obscure or solipsistic. True, he has admitted that he experienced an interval of personal discontentment and sterility after publishing *The Aunt's Story*; however, there were many forces at work in him at the time. Although he had at last accepted Australia as his home, he was not sympathetic with the literary patriots who were intent on glorifying swagmen, squatters, aborigines, blacks, and Chows. These zealots, White felt, were too solemn as they tried to develop an authentic Australian literature. He was much less sure of his own commitment, or at least he was sure that he did not share their commitment.

When White finally decided to write his own novel about a pioneering Australian family, his approach to the subject was more humanistic than historical; he was less interested in regional values than in those shared by all human beings. He was neither promoting a culture in ferment nor solving the problems of a colony becoming a nation. Above all, he was not trying to reconcile those irreconcilables that are part of the human condition. His attitude toward his material was minimally political. Furthermore, his idiom would not accommodate the kind of rationalism that differentiates errors in perception from facts. All perceptions, right or wrong, are significant for White, and unlike naturalists, who report only observables, he admits into court mysteries, intuitions, and even hallucinations as dependable evidence. White defines

and defends the significance of the meaning-at-the-moment
of an experience, whether the experience is one he imagines
for his characters or one he artfully arranges for the reader.
Technique in the way of rhetoric and imagery are for him
means to an artistic end, namely, to tell the whole truth.

White remembers that he often worked on *The Tree of
Man* at his kitchen table while suffering from attacks of
asthma. He says that he deliberately chose to write about "an
ordinary man and woman" in order to project "every possible aspect of life." The goal was an ambitious one, and he
knew that to reach it he would have to employ techniques
that would confuse some readers. It was his serious intention, he reports, "to discover the extraordinary behind the
ordinary, the mystery and the poetry which alone could
make bearable the lives of such people, and incidentally, my
own life since my return."[1]

Such a commitment entails many risks, including stylistic
obstacles to coherence. Thus attempts to reduce White's
writing to conventional communications—to simple sense,
as it were—often violate the artist's vision. The need to transcend pedestrian meanings is a genuine Patrick White hall-
mark. It puts him closer to the saints and the martyrs than is
comfortable for those who fear deviations. At this time
White realized that for him what once "had meant the prac-
tice of an art by a polished mind in civilised surroundings"
had now become "a struggle to create completely fresh
forms out of the rocks and sticks of words."[2]

Without false modesty, White began to accept the role of a
prophet. Prophets intend to tell the truth. Their utterances,
no matter how cryptic or enigmatic they may seem to skeptics, are intelligible to the faithful. Some converts study
White's fiction as seriously as theologians scan the pro-
nouncements of a deity, assuming always that the prophetic
message must be meaningful if one works hard enough to ex-
plicate it. White's commitment asks the reader to believe in
him, to trust that his words always signify. In fact, his impatience with many of his famous predecessors, such as
Goethe, whom he distrusted intensely, reflects his almost
narcissistic confidence in his own ability to write honestly.[3]

The Tree of Man (1955) and *Voss* (1957) are the first of

White's major works to reflect the author's determination not to condescend to the needs of mediocre readers and critics. They are controversial works precisely because White intended them to be. His acceptance of the elusiveness of wisdom such as he was reaching for allowed him to contradict himself and to violate rules of grammar and logic. He also began to emphasize human eccentricities as something more than amusing. Every White novel has a fair share of eccentric characters who are as entertaining as Charles Dickens's grotesques—with one big difference. While many of Dickens's humorous characters today appear to be psychotic and thus lose credibility, White's eccentrics often turn out to make more sense than the allegedly sane and reasonable people around them. Although their neighbors may shun them, their creator, the novelist, obviously loves them. In fact, White seems to urge the reader to rely on their inconsistencies as evidence of authenticity. For example, in his works atheists pray, illiterates verbalize eloquently, and primitives behave civilly. The reader relies on the writer to make him understand intuitively what intellect alone could not comprehend.

The Tree of Man

Patrick White's pioneer, Stan Parker, is given certain advantages from the beginning of the story.[4] He inherited a tract of uncleared land from his parents at an age when he was still young enough to exploit it fully. By the turn of the century Australia was beginning to prosper. A man could hope for at least modest success if he was willing to work hard.

Stan is handsome and strong although his strength is qualified by the authorial voice, which at once sets the tone of the hero's struggle with nature: "Life had not yet operated on his face. He was good to look at; also, it would seem, good. Because he had nothing to hide, he did perhaps appear to have forfeited a little of his strength. But that is the irony of honesty" (4). As a boy he had promised to "love God and never to touch a drop" although "he had had experience of neither, and the sun was in his eyes" (5). Later, still sun-blind, Stan marries Amy Fibbens as ingenuously as he had renounced liquor. He does not decide to marry her—"if decision implies pros and cons; he simply knew that he would do it, and as there was no reason why the marriage ceremony should be delayed, it was very soon performed . . ." (19).

The Parkers begin married life in a hand-made house set in a clearing which under the direction of Stan "encroached more and more on the trees . . ." (26). There Amy is often alone when Stan goes to market. Greedy for love, she finds company in her rosebush and in several neighbors, the O'Dowds and the Quigleys.

In time, storms, floods, and other natural disasters—those upheavals called acts of God—teach their own kinds of lessons. One day there is a great fire which destroys a nearby mansion built by the prosperous butcher, Mr. Armstrong. Stan heroically rescues the Armstrongs' beautiful house guest, Madeleine, the intended wife of handsome Tom Armstrong. As Stan carries the young woman from the flaming house, he goes through a complete cycle of lust, revulsion, passion, and agony. Amy, however, is unable to share Stan's ecstasy. His face remains closed to her as they walk home that evening through the providential rain, the rain that was too late to save the great house but did save the town.

When Australia enters World War I, Stan enlists at once, leaving his wife and two young children, Ray and Thelma, at home. His war experiences are condensed by the novelist into several letters to Amy. The most compelling event is his chance encounter on the field one day with a severed human hand: "The fingers of the lost hand were curled in its last act. It lay there like a tendril that had been torn off some vine, and dropped when the motive, if ever there was one, had been forgotten" (203). At that moment Stan remembers the hand of a priest raised in blessing, and he thinks "with increased longing of a God that reached down, supposedly, and lifted up. But he could not pray now. His stock of prayers, even his stock of improvisations, no longer fitted circumstances" (204).

When Stan returns home, he seems to accept the changes that have occurred during his absence, such as the maturing of his two children; yet he also remembers "acts of terror . . . [which] begin to illuminate the opposite goodness and serenity of the many faces of God'' (253).

During her middle age Amy's brief experiment with adultery with a traveling salesman soon fades into unimportance in her life although once on a rare visit to church she understands that she has sinned. Stan, who discovers the affair, reacts violently for a few days but the event is never discussed at home. The novelist remains noncommittal.

When Mrs. O'Dowd, Amy's neighbor and friend, dies of cancer, Amy is the inscrutable witness. Telling her husband about it that evening, Amy is characteristically laconic: "She is gone." This information is followed by silence and a "tea of chops and chips" (479). The old couple, the novelist writes, are "destitute even of each other" (479).

Resolutions

The dry authorial voice offers little comfort as character after character is disposed of more or less ignominiously. Madeleine, who first appears briefly as a vision of beauty to Amy and then as an erotic temptation to Stan during the great fire, disappears from the book until she reappears years later as Thelma's friend. She soon dies, however, and the reader is informed that the effect on Thelma is "an increase in loneliness" and the discovery "that her circulation was bad" (487). Only Doll Quigley rises to heights of true agony as she solves the problem of her dependent, half-witted brother by killing him; and in the sequel Doll frightens Amy: "I put him away," Doll explains. "I will not say kill." Amy is confused as she experiences a "fear and distaste for the blinding logic of Doll's act" (482). Amy's recognition of violence as logical is the keenest intellectual insight in her life, but she retreats at once from such dizziness.

Stan has already suffered a stroke when one afternoon, while resting in a chair outdoors, he is confronted by a young evangelist who crudely tries to save the old man's soul. Stan resists: "I am not sure whether I am intended to be saved." At that moment he also spits, partly because he is full of phlegm, partly because he wants to spit. He points to the "gob of spittle" on the ground before him and says: "That is God" (495). The evangelist is defeated and leaves. The dying

Stan then proclaims his creed—which is, of course, not necessarily the novelist's:

I believe, he said, in the cracks in the path. On which ants are massing, struggling up over an escarpment. But struggling. Like the painful sun in the icy sky. Whirling and whirling. But struggling. But joyful. So much so, he was trembling. The sky was blurred now. As he stood waiting for the flesh to be loosened on him, he prayed for greater clarity, and it became obvious as a hand. It was clear that One, and no other figure, is the answer to all sums. (497)

After Stan dies, Amy goes to "call those people who would come and give her material assistance. She promised herself great comfort from this. And from the grandson . . . in whose eyes her own obscure, mysterious life would grow transparent at last" (497).

The brief epilogue is a prose poem about that grandson and a piece of glass. As the boy is left looking "through the glass at the crimson mystery of the world" (498), the novelist has the last words: "So that in the end there were the trees. The boy walking through them with his head drooping as he increased in stature. Putting out shoots of green thought. So that, in the end, there was no end" (499).

A Hard, Worn Wisdom

William Walsh emphasizes the "hard, worn wisdom" that motivates Stan finally to equate God and a gob of spittle. Quite wisely, Walsh observes that the old man's remark is "not an observation capable of proof or disproof." Nevertheless, Walsh stresses the success of the novel "in establishing the palpable actuality of common life, and further in communicating the intimations of other realities which lie locked within quotidian experience."[5] Walsh may, however, have underestimated the irony in White's intentions.

White assigned the explanation of the title to the least sympathetic of his characters, Thelma Parker Forsdyke, whose marriage to her affluent but mediocre employer made her a lady of leisure with cultural pretensions. She often glances at a book with her tea. One day, upset by a visit from her brother, she comes across a poem and is attracted by the lines: "The tree of man was never quiet; / Then 'twas the

Roman, now 'tis I."[6] Thelma reads on because she suddenly realizes that it might "be knowledge, not aspirin or ephedrene, that will bring relief." It is not given to Thelma, however, to understand the poem completely although she does realize that she has apparently missed something in life: "Half sensing the meaning of the poem, she blamed her parents bitterly for the situation to which she had been exposed. She also blamed God for deceiving her" (390).

Thelma tries just once more to penetrate the meaning of her life. One day she happens to hear a great violinist perform a great concerto. The concerto, the novelist explains, "had really taken over the men who were brave enough to play it, and in some cases those who were listening. Thelma Forsdyke lowered her eyelids in the face of this assault, shocked and frightened by her approaching nobility." The novelist goes on to comment: "Almost anyone can be raised at some point in his life to heights he dare not own" (488–89). Thelma, however, retreats from the intensity of her feelings almost immediately and leaves the concert hall, "sucking a little cachou that she had had in her bag" (489).

In much the same way Amy and Stan are allowed only to approach understanding although they have many more and much deeper insightful moments than Thelma. However, Amy finally retreats fully: "In time the knowledge that some mystery was withheld from her ceased to make her angry, or miserable for her own void. She accepted her squat body, looking out from it . . . in dry acceptance of her isolation" (326). She survives Stan because she accepts her limitation sooner and more fully than Stan can accept his. When Stan speaks his final lines about God and spittle and the transcendental conclusion that One is the answer to all sums, he is near death as well as suffering from the aftereffects of a stroke. Despite the neatness of his answers to the inquisitorial man of God, Stan dies knowing it was too late for him to communicate even with Amy. Only the Parkers' grandson may be granted a fuller vision.

John McLaren calls Stan's limited final vision "typically numinous and vague." Nevertheless, he praises the novel for its conventionality, preferring it to *Voss* and *Riders in the Chariot,* which betray the reader into assuming deep values implicit in the "sentimental" symbolism. McLaren suggests that when the reader "comes to the end he is ashamed to admit that he has not understood it. So he supplies his own interpretation, and White gains another admirer." [7]

McLaren may have exaggerated the Emperor's clothes syndrome in White's admirers, but many of them do assume that the master can never be wrong. The comparatively simple structure of *The Tree of Man,* however, and the straightforward progression of the story, stimulate fewer complaints from critics. The novel was well received in the United States, where it was first published, although characteristically White distrusted popular acceptance as perhaps thoughtless and glib. Certainly he did not intend to suggest that lonely pioneers were always heroes, or that loneliness was easily cured. Nature remains relatively hostile and man's clearings only encroach on the trees gradually, often ineffectively. Nature's trees and the tree of man are never quiet.

There is enough "hard, worn wisdom" in the novel to please those who believe that experience is an effective teacher. Yet too many times a valiant character fails to reconcile his own sense of futility with his faith in an ultimately kind nature or a fair providence. Brian Kiernan's understanding of the novel is based on both knowledge and empathy and is relatively free of the Emperor's clothes fallacy. He concludes that the only affirmation at the end is in the epilogue, which turns over the job of "reconciling both struggle and joy" to the artist. [8] Stan was meant to fail to communicate, although he may have *felt* the reconciliation, his "gob of spittle" definition of God is ineffective—evidence of his inarticulateness rather than a brilliant metaphor.

Voss

For his next novel White adapted parts of a real-life adventure to his own idiom and commitment. He had become interested in the accounts of an early, failed expedition into the heart of the Australian darkness, which had been led by a fanatical German, Ludwig Leichhardt, whom he began to compare with Hitler. *Voss* was conceived, White remembers, during the Blitz while he was holed up in a bed-sitter in London. The novel is set in the 1840s, the time of Leichhardt's expedition, and was thus a challenge to White's impatience with typical historical romances, which all too often change trivial experiences into escape for casual readers. The "black in White" is given full scope in the work as well as the novelist's compassion for outsiders—outside because of intelligence, madness, or social status. The novelist honors some of the conventions of the nineteenth century, satirizes others, but all in all *Voss* is a twentieth-century work, reflecting White's personal preoccupation with the many faces and devices of providence.

Voss is a tightly constructed work. Divided into sixteen chapters, the time sequences are treated polyphonically rather than chronologically; that is, events happen simultaneously in different places—in different keys, as it were—so that the reader's awareness grows incrementally. Coincidences contribute to the feeling that somehow everything counts. No detail turns out to be merely padding; thus the "story" is not easy to summarize. Above all, *Voss* is not history.

The man called Voss first appears as a visitor in the affluent home of the upper-middle-class Bonner family near Sydney. He is announced by the maid as "a kind of foreign man" to Laura Trevelyan, the Bonners' niece. Laura realizes that the man calling upon her aunt and uncle, who are at church, "can only be the German." At that moment, the novelist confides, "her Sunday dress sighed."[9] Laura has not gone to church because she no longer believes in God: "How her defection has come about was problematic, unless it was by some obscure action of antennae, for she spoke to nobody who was not ignorant, and innocent, and kind." Nevertheless, Laura, like Stan in *The Tree of Man,* does believe in simple things. Instead of spittle, however, she believes in "wood . . . and in clear daylight, and in water" (5).

Laura is different from her relatives. The Bonners are of and by the upper-middle-class in mid-century Australia. Her uncle is described as "a merchant of great material kindness" whose affluence has helped soften many hardships for his family. His wife "had upholstered all hardnesses till she could sit on them in comfort." Their daughter, Belle, is young and "of a hilarious nature." Despite the good intentions around her, and partly because of them, Laura feels alone. But she is brave: ". . . in the absence of a rescue party, she had to be strong" (6).

When Voss enters the drawing room, he is offered, at Laura's direction, the second best port and some biscuits. Soon—too soon for propriety—Laura confides her origins to the stranger as they wait for the return of the family. She, too, is a kind of foreigner, having been born in England, orphaned early, and sent to live with her relatives in Australia. Threatened at first by Laura's seeming strength, Voss recovers when she confesses to certain weaknesses. A symbiotic relationship between the two begins as her weakness feeds his strength and gains its own strength when she realizes he needs her weakness to be strong.

The interplay continues, with Laura and Voss performing as if they were reading scripts about which they had serious doubts. When the maid brings refreshments, a third person in the room is reassuring: "Order does prevail" (8). Laura knows, however, that this order is temporary: "It was . . . but a transitory comfort. Voices, if only in whispers, must break in. Already she herself was threatening to disintegrate into the voices of the past" (8).

The leisurely introduction of Voss and Laura to each other and to the reader continues as Voss swallows a drop of wine, which for him at the moment is a complex event: "His throat was suddenly swelling with wine and distance, for he was rather given to melancholy at the highest pitch of pleasure, and would at times even encourage a struggle, so that he might watch" (9).

Voss sees that Laura is beautiful. At once she knows what he has seen and ruthlessly admits to herself that she is beautiful—"but fleetingly, in certain lights, at certain moments . . ." (10). Voss has, however, always considered himself free of the need for beautiful women, and Laura has had a similar delusion, having convinced herself that she is "contemptuous of men" (11). The two delusions are to crash head-on as the story progresses.

When the Bonner family returns from church Laura withdraws from further contact with Voss, even though she sees he is uncomfortable with the Bonners: "She personally could not assist. She had withdrawn. But nobody can help, she already knew" (12). The purpose of Voss's visit is to discuss his impending expedition into the dark interior of Australia. The wealthy Mr. Bonner is one of Voss's principal patrons. Voss explains that a ship will carry him and his party to Newcastle. Before they enter the wilderness on foot they will make a stop at Mr. Sanderson's ranch, "Rhine Towers," and a final stop at the last outpost, "Jildra." The members of the group who will accompany the explorer include Robarts, a young English lad; Le Mesurier, who "has great qualities, if he does not cut his throat"; Palfreyman, an ornithologist of "great principles"; and Turner, "a labourer" (17). When Bonner asks Voss if he is confident of their suitability, Voss answers evasively: "I am of every assurance that I can lead an expedition across this continent . . ." (17). Bonner then informs Voss that two more men will join him later: Angus, a rich young property owner; and Judd, a recently freed convict, "a man of physical strength and moral integrity" (18).

The Bonners invite Voss to stay for dinner, and when he refuses and leaves abruptly they condemn him as "nasty." The novelist stresses the adjective as Voss himself agrees: "All along the gritty road this nastiness was apparent to Voss himself. At such times he was the victim of his body, to which other people had returned him. So he walked furiously. He was not lame, but could have been" (22).

In a subsequent conference between Voss and three of his followers, Voss tries to define his own commitment. To Le Mesurier, who ostensibly is the brightest, the leader admits that he wants to cross the continent because he desires to know it with his heart: "Why I am pursued by this necessity," he says, "it is no more possible for me to tell than it is for you, who have made my acquaintance only before yesterday" (29). Le Mesurier appears to understand, but later when Voss predicts that Le Mesurier will immolate himself, Le Mesurier shouts: "You *are* mad." Whereupon Voss answers: "If you like" (31).

In contrast to Le Mesurier's doubts, Harry Robarts accepts Voss completely and "would have liked to touch his savior's skin" (34). Turner arrives drunk, and it is apparent that he will remain drunk most of the time. In his inebriation he adores Voss almost as much as Robarts does. Voss is re-assured and that night goes to bed, confident that no one "could damage the Idea . . . " (40). Early the next day, he confers with Palfreyman, the most religious member of the group. When Voss commends his strength of purpose, Palfreyman credits God's will. Voss responds ambivalently, with both envy and disgust. The novelist explains that Voss has identified Palfreyman as one of the "feminine men" who "merge themselves with the concept of their God . . . " (44).

During Laura's second encounter with Voss at a picnic she has a chance further to explore the German, whom she now sees as "vast and ugly" (83). Voss is aware of her verdict and tells her that he does not need her "good opinion," and ac-cuses her of "intellectual vanity" (84–85). He suggests that her vaunted atheism is self-centered and not like his own skepticism. He challenges a God "above humility" (85). Laura realizes the intensity of her feelings about Voss are a mixture of contempt and tenderness. Her final verdict: "He creates his own logic" (103). Thus she is not really surprised when after his departure she receives a letter from him pro-posing marriage. She answers at once, and her formal accep-tance reaches Voss just before he leaves Jildra. In her letter Laura identifies "mutual hatefulness" as the tie be-tween them and says that she is "prepared to wrestle" with that on the understanding that they "may *pray together* for salvation" (181). Laura's response seems to Voss all the more passionate for what it suppresses. Voss leads his men out of Jildra toward the dark interior of the continent confident that he will succeed.

Failure

As Laura has foreseen, however, the expedition follows its destined course into failure when loyalty patterns begin to shift. The group splits on a serious issue, namely, to believe in Voss's vision or to trust Judd's knowledge. Obviously the experienced Judd knows the wilderness better than Voss, and those not blinded by faith in Voss prefer Judd as leader. Although Voss claims to be called, Judd has realistic doubts about what Voss was called to do. Inevitably he helps reinforce Voss's self-image as a god. When Judd emerges as a betrayer—as Voss's Judas—Voss sees himself as the Savior. Meanwhile, the novelist exploits the daily events in the Bonner household as a counterpoint to the expedition's disasters. When a servant, Rose Portion, dies after giving birth to an illegitimate child, Laura adopts the little girl as her own. Obsessed with her role as surrogate mother, she eventually becomes mysteriously ill.

Laura's cousin, Belle, becomes the other center of activity when she marries. Although Belle is relatively insipid, she is one of the few fixed points in a shifting universe. Belle's wedding, her subsequent children, her acceptance of her officer-husband's mediocrity—out of uniform he loses his style—are all constants and are appropriately described in a low key.

As it becomes increasingly clear that Judd and Voss will separate, the passion in both narratives escalates. Belle's wedding marks the beginning of Laura's apotheosis: " . . . a bridesmaid who did not match the others" (325). At the same time Voss realizes that only a minority will follow him as he and Judd agree to part: "This was to be the test, then" (340). However, even before the split, when Palfreyman is killed by natives, Voss refuses to read the burial service for the dead man, and Judd announces that he cannot. After Angus, the rich man, reads a few words while Robarts sees the soul leave Palfreyman's body, Angus, Turner, and Judd go off together, leaving Le Mesurier, Robarts, and a native guide, Jackie, to follow Voss.

Those who stay with Voss soon become disciples, and each eventually assesses the credentials of his leader-savior. When they are captured by aborigines, Le Mesurier discovers that Voss has survival plans for himself only. The disillusioned man destroys a book of his poems and then slits his own throat. Robarts dies guarding the entrance to Voss's prison-tent. Jackie tries to remain loyal to Voss until he rediscovers his identification with the aborigines and then proves his new loyalty by beheading Voss with the penknife his master had lovingly given him in the beginning of their relationship.

Meanwhile, Laura's illness bewilders the Bonners, who cannot classify it. Voss's final behavior is also equivocal, allowing the reader to invent his own glosses. The text here insists on equivocation—the heart of any mystery. At the climax of her illness and of Voss's failure, Laura speaks, "It is over" (389). Her fever has broken and Laura has had her vision. Voss is dead. The relationship between Laura and Voss presumably transcended space as their constant awareness of each other is insisted upon by the novelist.

At a ceremony honoring the memory of the dead Voss, which takes place a number of years after the main events of the story, Laura meets and converses with members of the subsidiary set of characters who have survived along with Laura. They are largely home-town folks: a cousin, Willie Pringle; Colonel Hebden, who has tried to solve the mystery of the lost expedition; Mr. Sanderson, who had entertained Voss at Rhine Towers; and the ex-convict Judd, the only member of the expedition to return.

Laura is discontented with the bland statements of others and Judd's lies about closing Voss's eyes when Voss died. Laura's verdict is mild, and sad: "I am convinced that Voss had in him a little of Christ like other men. If he was composed of evil along with the good, he struggled with that evil. And failed" (438). When Laura's adopted daughter, Mercy, suggests to her mother that they "go into another room," Laura announces: "I will not go, I am here. I will stay." The novelist explains: "Thus she made her covenant" (439). Laura then suggests that Voss "did not die," and that if there is any need for proof, "the air will tell us. . . . " After this exalted moment, the last lines of the book return to the earth and dwindle to prose: "By which time she had grown hoarse, and fell to wondering aloud whether she had brought her lozenges" (442).

Among the Immortals

Voss demanded attention. William Walsh published a monograph on it in a prestigious series which put White among the immortals: Shakespeare, Milton, Pope, Austen, Fielding, and F. Scott Fitzgerald. Walsh found, quite properly and almost immediately, that *Voss* is an extraordinary novel, containing "not only a positive but also a negative revelation." Nevertheless, he cites faults, such as "the syntax bowled disconcertingly on the wrong foot. . . . "[10]

Serious interpretations of *Voss* either concentrate on the imagery or the symbols—or both—to extend the significance of the described action, events, and characters. Any "crossing" refers to the crucifixion, birds in flight to the soul, and thrones to the godhead. Also, the message of the book is allegedly multifold.

Sylvia Gzell identifies three themes common to *Voss* and White's next novel, *Riders in the Chariot*. She summarizes them as three searches: one for integrity, one for fulfillment, and one for transcendent understanding. White's "themes," she concludes, "are presented obliquely."[11] That obliqueness is one of White's most controversial characteristics, allowing the reader to project many of his own values and needs. Those hungry for spiritual solace respond positively to the mystifying complexities. Agnostics and skeptics are more reluctant to accept the obliqueness and the contradictions.

For example, an American critic angrily rejected the novel: "If this novel is anything more than a literary all-day sucker, the fact has been completely obscured by pretentious stylistic wrappings."[12] That Voss is a mad explorer but amazingly important to his faithful girl, who seems equally demented at times, is typical of the most drastic reductions of the plot. Elevations of the plot always canonize Voss, sometimes as a devil rather than a saint, but all reach willy-nilly for spiritual values. An example of a recent attempt to cast new light on old darkness is the thesis that "the Behmenist current in *Voss* tends to . . . provide a model for White's somewhat paradoxical view of the world; dark yet capable of redemption from within by the spontaneous conflict of spiritual principles."[13]

In general, the novel was considered quite difficult. Certainly it disturbed those readers who had cut their literary teeth on either Australian pulp fiction or the solemn stories of the social realists. Vance Palmer, for example, although literate and informed, had made a living writing popular novels for the pulp publisher, the N.S.W. Bookstall Company. His stories were designed "to exploit popular taste"

and "to appeal to the urban and rural masses," according to
Vivian Smith, who defines the genre: "Family feuds, conflict-
ing loyalties . . . romanticized rigors of droving . . . clear-cut
social divisions represented by the station and the shanty
—all these contributed to a form that is as definable as the
colonial romance from which it develops or degenerates."[14]

The pulps flourished in the 1920s, but even later when
Vance Palmer and his wife Nettie began to write for a less
commercial market, they continued to emphasize the Australian heritage. Australian history, literature, and criticism
were to shine with pride—and of course to be true. In contrast, White's *Voss* was not meant to be historically true.
Although set in Australia, it is not really a bush story nor is it
socially conscious. Admirers of Eleanor Dark's accurately
detailed settings were uncomfortable with White's cavalier
attitude toward geography and meteorology, for example.
Even Miles Franklin, whose prolonged absence from Australia in the middle of her life is a cloudy area, did not write
about experiences unfamiliar to Australians. She remained
strongly attached to the tradition represented by Joseph
Furphy. White, who was born the year Joseph Furphy died,
knew that he was different from his predecessors and most
of his contemporaries, although he was not entirely alone,
even in Australia, in his break with naturalism. He preferred,
however, to stand apart and expect the worst, distrusting
both friendly and hostile appraisals of his fiction at this time.

Chapter Five

Messages in Wheels and Marbles: *Riders in the Chariot* and *The Solid Mandala*

Patrick White's rejection in *The Tree of Man* and *Voss* of the realistic Australian novel was not, according to Ray Willbanks, quite unique. For example, Willbanks finds in several novels by the Australian writer, Randolph Stow, particularly in *A Haunted Land* (1956) and *To the Islands* (1958), the same phenomenon: "Instead of the observation of the outward man, these novelists turned inward. From the realistic approach, White and Stow moved to the romantic, the poetic; both writers began to explore their themes in terms of symbol and myth."[1]

Stow, who was born in 1935, has testified to White's influence, beginning with Stow's second novel. White helped liberate the younger man as well as others from "The Spell of the Bush" and "The Great Australian Dream," which were, according to T. Inglis Moore, two of the most popular patterns of concern in early Australian literature.[2] In the stories of these new writers adventures are subordinated to interiorized events. Journeys become spiritual quests in which failure on one level may mean success on another. White's *Voss*, for example, failed in reaching his ostensible goal but he did succeed in losing his pride. His discovery that he was not a god was a big step toward admitting the possibility that someone else or something else was supreme. In much the same way, Stow's protagonist in *To the Islands*, an old man who seeks the solace of the wilderness to expiate the crime of having killed a man, has come to distrust God. As a result, he confronts the ultimate absurdity in the universe. Near the end of his expiatory quest the old man explains the state of affairs to a friend: "Oh God . . . if there was a God this filthy Australian, British, human blood would have been dried up in me with a thunderbolt when I was born."[3]

White expected that at least some readers would understand his intentions in *The Tree of Man*—but he was not reassured by the immediate popularity of the work, especially in the United States where it was first published. The rave reviews were too glib and not always based on a careful and compassionate reading. Similarly, when later *Voss* was praised for the wrong reasons, White was even more annoyed. He remembers the event bitterly:

Half of those professing to admire *Voss* did so because they saw no connection between themselves and the Nineteenth Century society portrayed in the novel. As child-adults many Australians grow resentful on being forced to recognize themselves divorced from their dubious antiques, surrounded by the plastic garbage littering their back yards; they shy away from the deep end of the unconscious. So they cannot accept much of what I have written about the century in which we are living, as I turn my back on their gush about *Voss*.[4]

It would seem that sometimes White needs to be misunderstood by those he has judged incapable of understanding him as a reassurance that his writing is indeed authentic. He has asked to be tried in higher courts than those represented by his suburban neighbors, most of whom could not distinguish between plastic copies and the real thing.

Riders in the Chariot

Patrick White's sixth novel is the product of a mature writer speaking in his own voice. In *Riders in the Chariot* the novelist makes no attempt to conceal his acceptance of his role as a latter-day prophet. The theme-announcing epigraph is from William Blake, a passage in which the Old Testament prophets, Isaiah and Ezekiel, define their perceptions of God. Isaiah calls the voice of God "the voice of honest indignation," admitting that he has neither seen nor heard God "in a finite organical perception." His "senses," however, had "discover'd the infinite in everything. . . . " Ezekiel, in the same mode, avoids specifics and defends his own eccentric behavior—eating dung and lying on his right and left sides for immoderately long intervals—as the result of his desire to raise "other men into perception of the infinite."[5]

In accord with the themes suggested by the epigraphs, White set for himself the task of doing what Holstius had told Theodora to do in *The Aunt's Story*, namely, to accept irreconcilables and then to go on from there. To project this message the novelist must persuade his readers that irreconcilables are no barrier to perceiving the infinite. In fact, irreconcilables are a help rather than a hindrance. Only a prophet would dare thus to confound logic and to defend excesses as spiritually therapeutic. White's equivalent of eating dung and lying on his right and left sides immoderately long is verbal. His lofty rhetoric, fractured syntax, and reckless imagery are defensible only if such excesses work. Beginning with *Riders in the Chariot* White has dared to believe he can make them work.

The major metaphor, the Chariot, comes from the Book of Ezekiel in the Old Testament, although details are altered and adapted to fit the four "Riders" in the novel. Other chariots are subsumed in the central image, such as the Cabalistic, Buddhist, and Tarot, as well as many other chariots of myths, folklore, and fairy tales. White specifies his indeterminate use of the metaphor about one-third way through the novel. One of the four Riders, a Professor Mordecai Himmelfarb, has been researching chariots in "old books and manuscripts" (141). One evening he begins to scribble, discovers he has drawn a chariot. When his wife asks him which chariot he has drawn, he answers:

That I am not sure. . . . It is difficult to distinguish. Just when I think I have understood, I discover some fresh form—so many—streaming with implications. There is the Throne of God, for instance. That is obvious enough—all gold, and chrysoprase, and jasper. Then there is the Chariot of Redemption, much more shadowy, poignant, personal. And the faces of the riders. I cannot begin to see the expression of the faces. (142)

The symbol may be shadowy and even irresolutely used but White's quartet of *illuminati* are fully realized in Mary Hare, Mordecai Himmelfarb, Ruth Godbold, and Alf Dubbo. When the story opens, Mary Hare, an elderly and impoverished spinster, has just engaged a housekeeper for Xanadu, her decaying ancestral home, the possibility of doing so having occurred to her at the resumption of a small allowance from a distant relative. She is apprehensive about this good luck, and she is not surprised when her new housekeeper, with the ominous name of Mrs. Jolley, soon begins to bully her. One day, after a quarrel, Mrs. Jolley presents her with a pink cake inscribed: "FOR A BAD GIRL." Miss Hare praises the cake "with something like horror" as Mrs. Jolley "lowers her eye-lids." At the moment Miss Hare senses "some danger to the incorporeal, the more significant part of her" (60). In a word, Mrs. Jolley is evil.

Miss Hare, in contrast, is essentially good and thus vulnerable. She lives close to the ground, glides through bushes easily, and has become in her old age an eccentric in the neighborhood. As she slowly emerges in the story, she relates to the other three Riders one by one as the novelist introduces them. The first is Ruth Godbold. Miss Hare has "come up to the edge of the road, in search of something, whether child, goat, or perhaps just the daily paper" (3–4). Her neighbor, Mrs. Godbold, warns her: "You could get torn." Miss Hare agrees: "Oh, I could get torn. . . . But what is a little tear?" (4). The novelist comments:

It did not matter to either that much would remain unexplained. It did not matter that neither had looked at the other's face, for each was aware that the moment could yield no more than they already knew. Somewhere in the past, that particular relationship had been fully ratified. (4)

Mrs. Godbold was born Ruth Joyner and had served as a maid in her youth. She is now the wife of a drunkard and the mother of a brood of children. In contrast to the other Riders, who are often mistaken for insane because of their passions and eccentricities, Mrs. Godbold has been accepted by her neighbors as virtuous and dependable. Years later her former employer remembers her as "the rock of love" (525). She is built to endure. Her quiet and untutored intelligence illuminates and purges.

One day Miss Hare meets the third Rider, Himmelfarb. The scene is stark and stunning. She first sees him sitting under her plum tree: "She could have swum for ever on her wave, towards the island of her tree, holding out her hands, no longer begging for rescue, but in recognition" (91).

Himmelfarb at once responds to her happy mood and introduces himself. Soon he begins to tell her his life story. Born in North Germany, he was the right age and in the right place to experience the consequences of being Jewish. Even before World War I the boy remembers Russian relatives stopping at the prosperous Himmelfarb home on their way to America, fleeing pogroms not yet credible in Germany. Despite his skepticism, young Mordecai enlists in World War I, is wounded twice, and is awarded a medal. After the war he takes the doctorate degree, and his training as an intellectual makes it necessary for him to try to understand as the Nazi horror begins to intrude everywhere. One day he unintentionally saves his own life by visiting gentile friends on the evening the police raid the ghetto and take his wife prisoner.

As Miss Hare listens to Himmelfarb's story she realizes that he too knows about the Chariot. In answer to her questions he expresses his own confusion about the Riders. Perhaps they are the thirty-six holy men identified in the Hebraic tradition. His anxiety, however, is momentarily lessened as he and his new friend continue to sit together under the leafy canopy. He concludes his life story, telling how old friends gave him sanctuary until they too were eventually apprehended. He never finds his wife again, and although he is eventually also imprisoned, he miraculously escapes and is finally transported to Australia.

Miss Hare has also become increasingly interested in the appearance and behavior of a black man whom she has encountered now and then on her walks around Sarsaparilla: "He was all bones, and might have seemed to shamble, if it had not been for a certain convinced bearing" (62–63). She notices, however, that his shoulders are "at peace" (63).

Himmelfarb is also interested in the strange black man, whom he meets one day in the washroom of Rosetree's bicycle factory where they are both employed. There Himmelfarb discovers that his fellow worker is also familiar with Ezekiel's description of the Chariot, and that he is an Australian aborigine named Alf Dubbo. Raised and educated as an experiment by the Reverend Timothy Calderon and his maiden sister, the "abo" early shows signs of artistic talent. His sketches, however, are too bizarre for his patrons. Dubbo runs away when the Reverend seduces him. His subsequent adventures include an interlude living in a rubbish dump and affairs with two casual women, and the contracting of a venereal disease. All in all, however, White projects him as a fulfilled person: "Alf Dubbo was fortunate in that he had his fire, and would close his eyes, and let it play across his mind in those unearthly colours which he loved to reproduce" (377).

When Hannah, his current mistress, one day gives him an old Bible, he devours it at once: "The voices of the prophets intoxicated him as he had never been in his life, and soon he was laying on the grave splendour of their words with the colours of his mind" (379). But Hannah sells several of his pictures. He beats her, trashes his room, and leaves. Not long after that he goes to work at Rosetree's factory and eventually meets the other three Riders. His first encounter with Mrs. Godbold is especially spectacular.

One night Mrs. Godbold visits the local whorehouse, an unpretentious family affair, to fetch her husband home. The incident is both comic and poignant, for Mrs. Godbold's innocence is of the most sophisticated kind: "She no longer blamed her husband, altogether. She blamed herself for understanding" (296). She is waiting for her husband, Tom, to conclude his business with the whore when a black man enters the small living-waiting room of the establishment. The homey whore-mistress addresses him informally: "You dirty, drunken bastard," she shouts. "Didn't I tellya we was not accepting any further visits?" (297).

Mrs. Godbold, sitting quietly, is surprised at the fellow's answer: "This is no visit. This is a mission" (297). "A mission of love," he explains when asked; nevertheless, he is denied admission. Valiantly he begins to dance. He explains: "Because I am compelled to" (298). When in the excitement the dancer falls to the floor, Mrs. Godbold wipes his wound with her handkerchief.

"Are you comfortable?" she asks him. And the novelist adds: "As if he was a human being" (302).

The Wounding and the Healing

After establishing the four Riders as special characters, the novelist begins to activate them. Subsequent events are ordeals that test the Riders' credentials. Himmelfarb is the first to be tried. His employer, Mr. Rosetree—born Rosenbaum—is a convert to Christianity, something that Himmelfarb can only faintly understand. One night, alone at Passover time, Himmelfarb sets the Seder table and ritualistically opens his door to admit a stranger. He soon realizes that *he* is the stranger, and so he goes to join the Rosetrees' celebration as *their* stranger. He is coolly received, however, and returns to "the disaster of his [own] Seder table . . . the tomb of all those, including himself, who had not survived the return journey, and he, risen from the dead, the keeper of it" (424).

One day soon thereafter Himmelfarb arises early and prays the old prayers. He is described eloquently: "His veins were lapis lazuli in a sea of gold, the thongs of the phylacteries were turned to onyx, but the words that fell from his mouth were leaping crystals, each reflecting to infinity the words contained within the words" (429). Later that day at the factory, workers led by Blue, the son of Mrs. Flack, Mrs. Jolley's companion in evil, mockingly try to crucify Himmelfarb. They string him up in a tree in the factory yard as Dubbo watches: "Now Dubbo knew that he would never, never act, that he would dream, and suffer, and express some of that suffering in paint—but was, in the end, powerless. In his innocence, he blamed his darker skin" (441).

As Himmelfarb hangs there, hoisted up by his wrists, the novelist commands attention to the moment: "Those who had remained in touch with reality or tradition might have taken him for dead. But the eyes were visionary rather than fixed. The contemplative mouth dwelled on some breathless word spoken by the mind" (443). Although Himmelfarb is soon rescued, and the incident is written off as a prank, he leaves "the factory in which it had not been accorded to him to expiate the sins of the world" (449). No one, the novelist seems to say, can ever expiate that much sin.

One night not long after the mock hanging, the Jew's house is set on fire. "I do like a fire," Mrs. Jolley remarks to her friend, Mrs. Flack, upon catching sight of the "glow" in the sky (450). Miss Hare also sees the fire: "It was too jubilant to ignore, blaring out, trumpet-shaped, from amongst the deciduous exotics and shabbier native trees" (452). She knows that it is the Jew's house that is burning and that Blue is the arsonist. When she enters the burning house to rescue Himmelfarb, she cannot find him, and she emerges with her straw hat a flaming halo and her clothes on fire. She is not, however, consumed by the flames. The Jew, for the moment, is also safe in the home of Mrs. Godbold, fetched down there by the good woman shortly before the fire was set. When Miss Hare joins the group around the survivor, who is lying in Mrs. Godbold's bed, without hesitating she lies down across the Jew's feet to warm them.

Dubbo arrives later and, timidly peering through "the window, he did not think he could survive this Deposition, which, finally he had conceived. . . . So he went away as he had come" (469).

Himmelfarb dies on Good Friday and is conventionally buried, as Mrs. Godbold tells Rosetree, who has come to inquire: "Like any Christian" (479). Despondent and frightened, Rosetree goes home and hangs himself, fulfilling his role as an unwitting Judas. Meanwhile, Dubbo paints his last two pictures. In the first he depicts Himmelfarb as the Messiah, Mrs. Godbold and Mary Hare as the two Marys. In the second painting "the Chariot was shyly offered" together with "The Four Living Creatures" (494). His work completed, Dubbo also dies, hemorrhaging over his hands, which are described as "gilded . . . with his own gold" (494).

Miss Hare leaves the town after the Jew's death and is never seen again. When her home, Xanadu, is razed, a young laborer, picking out an old fan he has found in the ruins, dances a dance of death and of life as others watch him: "For the audience, his lithe thighs introduced an obscenity of life into the dead house" (503).

In the end Mrs. Jolley goes to live with her friend Mrs. Flack, who had planned most of the evil in the novel. The two will torment each other over endless cups of tea for as long as they live.

Only Mrs. Godbold survives intact: "Now she could approach her work of living, as an artist, after an interval, will approach and judge his work of art. . . . She was content to leave then, since all converged finally upon the Risen Christ, and her own eyes had confirmed that the wounds were healed" (531).

Wheels within Wheels

Riders in the Chariot has remained one of White's most controversial novels, for it is not an easy work to add up. The exaltation of the visionaries is mixed with acrid indictments of much that seemed plastic and ugly to the novelist, with the paradoxical result that what White was predisposed to glorify sometimes seems less real than the mediocrities and platitudes of the dullards. Such a paradox may be unavoidable, for goodness is by definition less blatant than evil. Brian Kiernan concludes that the novel "presents a deeply divided vision. Through his seers, the author explores different, yet only partial, paths to perception." Although the novelist has expressed "tensions between man's aspirations towards transcendence and the social world which denies these but in which he must still live, White is not so much resolving them as releasing them with great imaginative power and passion." Kiernan then qualifies the virtue of the passion: "A passion which at the same time prevents his achieving a sure control over his dramatic presentation of the conflict."[6]

What price passion if it vitiates control? Also, what price control if it attenuates passion? J. F. Burrows concludes that "there are too many questions of importance on which the novel never makes up its mind." He notes that in "the

Crucifixion-episode . . . White is seeking to express at once the Judaism of Himmelfarb, the revived Christianity of Dubbo, the grinding tension between Judaism and Christianity that is destroying Rosetree, and the xenophobia of the Sarsaparillan mob."[7]

William Walsh, whose partisanship is honest, accepts the fact that all four Riders fail, that "their lives are completed by ruin." But for him such failure signifies the novelist's success: "In each of these," he concludes, "this extraordinary novel confirms, there is achieved the success the world hates and needs."[8] Other critics deflect their own egos off White's. In 1962 an Australian critic declaimed with sly enthusiasm: "Here stands a work of art of great relevance to our time, and of great power, ranging from the design of outrageous hats for women [one lady wears a hat in the shape of an *active* volcano: it actually smokes] to visions of the Apocalypse."[9] Another reviewer, at the edge of understanding, complained that "White finds words more real than people."[10] An obvious rejoinder to this opinion is in order: Certainly literature begins and ends as words. Anyway, White's next novel came as a relief to those who must decode and decipher. It is easier to find messages in marbles than in so many wheels within wheels.

The Solid Mandala

The Solid Mandala is less complex than *Riders in the Chariot*.[11] For one thing, the central metaphor is less equivocal than the mysterious chariot and its ecstatic riders. In its simplest form a mandala is a circle enclosing a square. While the outer circle constrains, the inner square seems to strive to escape. A solid mandala is three-dimensional; in its simplest form it is a sphere enclosing a cube. The cube, however, may add striations of color or become a randomized shape, such as one finds in glass marbles and paperweights.

The psychologist Jung was interested in mandalas and assumed that they revealed much about their creators' unconscious processes. He also accepted the possible religious significance of these intricate patterns. An authentic mandala, by the addition of religious symbols, allegedly points the way to God. Jung warned the unwary, however, that mandalas can sometimes betray the seeker after spirituality. Contemplating one too long or in the wrong way can induce narcoses rather than epiphanies. True mandalas are not playthings. White allows the definition and relevance of his use of the mandala to remain indefinite until about halfway through the novel when Arthur Brown, one of the twin brothers who dominate the story, finds the definition of a mandala in a friend's encyclopedia, which he reads aloud:

> *" 'The Mandala is a symbol of totality. It is believed to be the "dwelling of the god." Its protective circle is a pattern of order super—imposed on—psychic—chaos. Sometimes its geometric form is seen as a vision (either waking or in a dream) or—'"*
> His voice had fallen to the most elaborate hush.
> *" 'Or danced,' "* Arthur read. (229)

The novel is divided into four parts, the first and fourth parts framing the second and third parts. The body of the novel consists of two long flashbacks in which the histories of the main characters, twin brothers, are explicated and dramatized both together and individually. The four-part structure and the central search for the meaning of the novel, which the novel self-consciously pursues, make it resemble a solid mandala.

The central story concerns the adventures and misadventures of the twin brothers, Waldo and Arthur Brown. The setting is largely confined to White's fictitious Sarsaparilla, which gives the author the opportunity to introduce an assortment of Australian suburbanites, among whom there are fewer enlightened souls than dullards. Nevertheless, the cast of characters is large and varied, with minor personalities sometimes making major contributions to the action.

The twins first appear as two old men walking hand in hand along the highway between Sarsaparilla and a larger city, Barranguli. Waldo and Arthur are observed from the window of a bus which is returning Mrs. Poulter and Mrs. Dun from a shopping trip to Barranguli, where there are more stores and more excitement than in the smaller suburb. Mrs. Dun, an anxious, dull woman relatively new to the neighborhood, does not know the old men. When she voices

her disapproval of men holding hands, Mrs. Poulter sighs
and defends the men: "They are old. . . . I expect it helps
them. Twins too" (11). Mrs. Poulter is at once established as
one of White's sympathetic characters. Like Mrs. Godbold
she will endure. Mrs. Dun, however, will never understand,
and she predicts that something horrible will happen.

The second part of the novel explores Waldo's "perspectives," a word which is more precise than "point of view,"
for the novelist adds selected perspectives of Arthur's. The
reader at first believes that he is being told everything about
Waldo; nevertheless, after some pages he begins to feel
uneasy about Waldo's expressed attitudes. He begins to
distrust not Waldo as much as the novelist himself. For example, Arthur remains passive, speaks little, and the reader
is seldom told what Arthur is thinking. The suggestion that
Arthur is not thinking at all follows the omission of "he
thoughts." Actually, Arthur has been thinking intensely all
along—in his own way—as the reader learns later.

On the day the two old men take their walk Waldo has
long been retired from his job as librarian, and Arthur also
from his more mundane job as a "helper." Both have tried
unsuccessfully to make adjustments to the situation. When
Waldo expresses his disappointment in not having succeeded
in becoming a writer, Arthur tries to persuade Waldo that
there is still time and plenty to write about. When he suggests that Waldo write about Mr. Saporta, the man whom
their mutual friend Dulcie has married, and about the carpets
that Saporta sells in his shop, "and all the fennel down the
side roads" (24), Waldo is annoyed, thinking to himself how
dull his brother is, and how "he had hoped originally for
intellectual companions with whom to exchange the Every-
man classics and play Schubert after tea" (24).

The story soon reverts to the childhood of the twins,
when their parents were still alive. Their mother was born in
England and immigrated when she married a rebel against
the decadent Anglo civilization. The twins' parents consider
themselves conscientious and liberated, but as they try to explain the twins, their only children, to friends, it is clear that
their perceptions are unreliable. In the parents' opinion
Arthur is handsome and healthy but retarded while Waldo,

although born weaker and smaller, has recovered and is now mentally superior.

The Truth about Arthur

The third part of the novel explores Arthur's character and projects a different version of reality. It now becomes increasingly clear that Arthur is more sensitive and intuitively intelligent than his brother. He is not the person he seems to be when, in the second part of the novel—Waldo's part—he appears one day in the library where Waldo works. Arthur has gone there to read *The Brothers Karamazov*. When he tries to tell Waldo, who pretends not to know him, that he does not understand the behavior of the Grand Inquisitor in Ivan's fantasy, Waldo evicts him from the library as if he were an alien, which indeed he seems to be at the time. Nothing more comes of the incident in that section.

In Arthur's part, the scene is replayed with a big difference, for the novelist is now obligated to tell what Arthur is thinking as well as what he is saying and doing when his brother discovers him in the library. Arthur is now the center of the novelist's concern: "Reading *The Brothers Karamazov* he wished he could understand whose side anyone was on," the novelist explains (274). Arthur understands the action but is not sure he grasps the meaning of the famous parable, although he senses it is relevant to his own anxiety. In Ivan's fantasy the Grand Inquisitor threatens to have Christ executed upon his return to earth as dangerous to the church. Christ had refused to satisfy humanity's craving for bread and miracles, leaving men free—and anxious. The church, in contrast, has provided the security of enslavement.

Presumably it is at this point in his reading that Arthur is rudely evicted by Waldo. The moment, Arthur knows, is decisive: "Afterwards Arthur could not remember in detail what was said. You couldn't exactly say *they* were *speaking,* because the remarks were being torn out of them helterskelter, between tears and gusts of breathlessness, like handfuls of flesh" (274). Arthur then realizes that both he and Waldo are lost, for there is not enough love to redeem them both. Like Christ's, his mission has been perverted.

Later in his part, Arthur "dances a mandala" for his neighbor-friend, Mrs. Poulter, who is at peace with the collective unconscious, as Jungian psychologists would say. Arthur trusts her, and during the dance, Mrs. Poulter is deeply moved. The first corner of Arthur's dance is his own and "a prelude to all that he had to reveal. . . . " There he dances "the dance of himself. Half clumsy, half electric . . . the gods dying on a field of crimson velvet, against the discords of human voices" (256).

In the second corner the inspired performer dances "his love for Dulcie Feinstein, and for her husband, by whom, through their love for Dulcie, he was equally possessed, so they were all three united, and their children still to be conceived. Into their corner of his mandala he wove their Star, on which their three cornered relationship was partly based" (256).

In the third corner Arthur dances his friend Mrs. Poulter, reaching for and attaining communion with her spirit. In the fourth corner he tries to dance his brother, but this corner gives Arthur trouble: "He couldn't dance his brother out of him, not fully. They were too close for it to work, closest and farthest when, with both his arms, he held them together, his fingers running with candle-wax. He could not save." So he merely "trampled the grass into a desert" (257).

The dance of the center, which is the last dance, belongs to Arthur and Mrs. Poulter. He dances the "passion of all their lives, the blood running out of the backs of his hands, water out of the hole in his ribs. His mouth was a silent hole, because no sound was needed to explain" (257).

When, near the end of the novel, Waldo ridicules a poem by Arthur, and Arthur in turn happens to catch Waldo dressed in their mother's clothes, the alienation between the two climaxes with the attempted murder of Arthur by Waldo and the inadvertent killing of Waldo by Arthur. The interpretation of these final and quickly narrated but significant events as seen from Arthur's perspective is apparently the authentic version; that is, the second version escalating with its passion and Arthur's authentic anguish is definitive.

In the end Arthur realizes that he has blasphemed: "Not so

much against God—he could understand God at a pinch—
but against the always altering face of the figure nailed on the
tree'' (284). Then Arthur kills his brother at the moment of
insight, the same moment in which Waldo tries to kill him
''in the agony of their joint discovery'' (284).

After killing Waldo, Arthur runs away from home. First he
peeks in on Dulcie and her family but dares not enter there.
In desperation he seeks out Mrs. Poulter. With her, in a quiet
interval, he hears the shots denoting the killing of the two
dogs that had been consuming the corpse of his brother.
Although at the time no explanation is given for the shots, he
seems to know. He weeps as Mrs. Poulter tells him she
believes in him. The novelist quickly certifies Mrs. Poulter's
statement: ''So she did, this man and child, since her God
was brought crashing down'' (304).

Although God has been brought crashing down, love remains. Mrs. Poulter says to the Sergeant who has come for
Arthur: ''This man would be my saint if we could still believe
in saints. Nowadays . . . we've only men to believe in. I
believe in this man'' (307). The arresting officer is kind. Mrs.
Poulter promises to visit Arthur, who hopes to be moved
eventually to a rest home called ''Peaches and Plums.''

The novel then ends quietly, all passion spent. When that
evening Mr. Poulter asks his wife about the news, she
hesitates before assuring her husband that nothing cata-
strophic has happened.

A Happy Hunting Ground

Arthur Brown's most cherished possessions were four
glass marbles, the kind that resemble solid mandalas. Eventually he gives one of them to his friend, Dulcie Feinstein,
the girl who marries the rug merchant; and one to his dear
friend, Mrs. Poulter, who is his spiritual alter ego. He offers
one, the inferior one of the four, to his brother, who refuses
to accept it, and he keeps the fourth one for himself. These
gifts suggest some meaning more esoteric than good-natured
sharing. Arthur's quartet of marbles—minus one leaves a
trinity—is a kind of super-mandala, at least to Arthur. Only
an elected is offered one part of four; only the eligible accept.

Waldo was elected in the eyes of Arthur but he scorned his marble-gift as a mere toy. He proved to be ineligible, so Arthur, Dulcie, and Mrs. Poulter remain the *illuminati.*

The whole novel, not only these bits and pieces of symbols, has become a happy hunting ground for mystics, Jungian psychologists, and collectors of marbles. One review, entitled "Messages in Marbles," rejoices in White's obscurities and paradoxes and notes that the novel keeps the reader "constantly interested and surprised."[12] Other critics and reviewers recognize, often with awe, the "arcane complications" in the novel.[13] Fossickers after higher and deeper truths welcome problems and are not baffled by stylistic knots, untying them eagerly to explain the messages inside the package: " . . . the technique of the novel . . . is exquisitely in symmetry with the central theme of the novel—the existence of a party of goodness and being, and the singular and profound secret unity which binds its members together."[14] Another interpretation accepts the mandala image as "an aspiration toward wholeness and integrity" but concludes that "the novel's parts do not add up to the whole."[15]

Patricia A. Morley, who enthusiastically supports the thesis that White is essentially a mystic, is somewhat troubled about the ending, especially about Mrs. Poulter's skepticism. Morley valiantly tries to resolve the problem: "Mrs. Poulter's apparent repudiation of her religion, the fact that Waldo's death means to her that 'her God was brought crashing down' and 'her Lord and master Jesus had destroyed Himself the same day' must be seen within the total context of the part which contains it and of the entire novel. . . . White's vision, unlike the numerous Christian heresies which hold that Christ's body was either a phantom or of celestial substance, affirms the full humanity of Christ and the substantial reality of his human body."[16]

White testifies in *Flaws in the Glass* to his own anxiety at the time he was writing *The Solid Mandala.* He and his friend Lascaris had decided to move from "Dogwoods," their home of many years, because the suburban nuisances were becoming oppressive. He feared that the uprooting might be fatal to his writing, that *The Solid Mandala* might be his "swan song." Inevitably the novel "was infused with an amount of fatality and foreboding." Furthermore, for those interested in the sources of White's inspiration and possible prototypes of his characters, he identifies the Brown twins as "my two halves," with Waldo as "myself at my coldest and worst." Mrs. Poulter "grew out of" a neighbor lady, and Dulcie "has both the goodness and the smugness of a fulfilled Jewish acquaintance."[17]

Apparently the novel is less mysterious than many critics assume!

Chapter Six

The Unprofessed Factor: *The Vivisector* and *The Eye of the Storm*

By the time White began to work on his eighth novel, *The Vivisector*, he had become aware of his implied readers. Peter Beatson quotes a statement White made in 1970 to Clem Semmler, in which the novelist identifies his objectives:

> I suppose what I am increasingly intent on trying to do . . . is to give professed unbelievers glimpses of their own unprofessed factor. I believe most people have a religious factor, but are afraid that by admitting it they will forfeit their right to be considered intellectuals. This is particularly common in Australia where the intellectual is a comparatively recent phenomenon. The churches defeat their own aims, I feel, through the banality of their approach, and by rejecting so much that is sordid and shocking which can still be related to religious experience . . . [*sic*] I feel that the moral flaws in myself are more than anything my creative source.
>
> This is what I am trying to do, more than before in *The Vivisector*, which is coming out this year. . . . [*sic*] the novel I am working on at present [*The Eye of the Storm*] . . . [*sic*] seems to have a more specifically religious content and pattern than the others.[1]

Beatson hopes to fit White into a less humanistic straitjacket when he goes on to stress the evil in White's characters as a theological necessity:

> Good and evil are both laws of necessity that operate in the fallen world. Since it is only by passing through and experiencing inwardly all the conditions of matter that the soul can reach God, it is necessary that characters should have subjective experience of

both. . . . Without such an experience the soul remains "once-born." Evil is an essential dynamic principle of spiritual growth. . . . [2]

Beatson's defense of White's use of sinful characters is ingenious but, despite the novelist's admission that he was becoming increasingly interested in arousing his reader's conscience, many sins committed by his favorite characters remain either attractive or amusing, and such characters are still headed for an orthodox damnation when White has finished with them. The artist, Hurtle Duffield, in *The Vivisector*, and the elderly widow, Elizabeth Hunter, in *The Eye of the Storm*, remain morally flawed. They are unbelievers who may have experiences that give them glimpses of White's "unprofessed factor," yet they are never fully redeemed. They die in sin because they are not truly penitent. Moral flaws, to White, can be the source of creative activity, as he tries to demonstrate in his eighth novel.

The Vivisector

The Vivisector is, technically at least, more advanced than its predecessors in White's canon. It extends the range of the uses of imagery and scrambled syntax as it probes the reader's conscience. It defends artistic license and redefines sanity. It is also White's dirtiest novel. Patricia Morley, whose faith in White is a leap, admits that the novel exhibits "an obsessive preoccupation with snot, spit, spilled semen, dung, vomit, dandruff, blackheads, foul breath, grease, sweat, farts, rats, flies—in a word, with things rancid and rotting and putrid."[3] Nevertheless, she finds the work therapeutic.

White named his protagonist Hurtle, a name which suggests both violence and wounds. Hurtle hurts and reacts violently because he experiences intensely the "great discrepancy between aesthetic truth and sleazy reality."[4] Once in a conversation with an ordinary person, a grocer, Hurtle calls God the "Divine Vivisector." The grocer, who is equipped with conventional sensors and conventional perceptions, does not understand. "Though he hadn't understood, it chilled the grocer: he could feel it trickling down his back" (235).

As a young boy Hurtle Duffield was literally sold to the
wealthy and worldly Mr. and Mrs. Courtney. Hurtle's
mother was Mrs. Courtney's laundress, and when Hurtle, a
precocious lad, seemed to Mrs. Courtney a potential genius,
she arranged to adopt him. Before that, however, Hurtle's
brief experience in an ordinary school with an unimaginative
teacher signals how different he is from others. At the age of
six he writes his autobiography for his teacher, Miss Adams,
who "looked as though she had a headache" (34). The boy
confesses in the composition that he is "droring a picture
which will be a shandeleer with the wind through it when it
is finished" (33). When asked what the picture means, he
refuses to explain, for "a shandeleer" is "his secret thing"
(34). He has also offended his mother by drawing a picture
which she calls the "Mad Eye." She complains that "it looks
right through you" (64). After that she is willing to sell the
strange boy.

After the Courtneys pay a decent sum of money as well as
arrange adoption legalities, Hurtle goes to live in his new
home, which includes the Courtneys' frail and deformed
daughter, Rhoda. He is uneasy at first but finds immediate
pleasure in exploring the Courtneys' paintings: "He would
have liked to lick the tempting paint, but the painting was
hung beyond reach of his tongue. He could only stand on the
leather-bottomed chair pulling his tongue in and out in an
imitation of licking" (51).

When Hurtle is twelve years old, "Maman" Courtney
takes the family to Europe. In London Maman reveals her
hatred of vivisectionists, introducing the first of several ex-
planations of the title of the novel. Noticing an anti-
vivisection display of a "little brown stuffed dog clamped to
a kind of operating table" in a store window, Maman reacts
emotionally, attracting passersby: "There's nothing so in-
human as a human being," she announces, then adds: "We
must never rest" (119). When Hurtle is frightened by her excessive reaction, Maman decides they must all go home at
once, observing that only Hurtle has learned anything on the
trip: "He's learned better ways of being nasty" (122).

From then on Hurtle realizes that few people will ever
understand him. Back home he is despised by his peers be-

cause he can speak British English and admired only because he has been to Paris. His foster mother accuses him of never forgiving others. Hurtle does not agree: "Himself the weakest, if he could have convinced her" (139). While Father is away from home, Maman moves in closer. In the catalytic event Maman embraces Hurtle: "She began gulping at his mouth: they were devouring with their two mouths a swelling, overripened, suddenly sickening—pulp" (148). Hurtle resists and goes off to fight in the newly declared war.

The Search

After the Armistice Hurtle decides to remain in Paris, washing "dishes by night to justify himself by day . . ." (159). Discarding the name Courtney, he begins to search for his true self. Later, when Maman Courtney, recently widowed, marries a young man who was earmarked for Rhoda and disinherits Hurtle, he knows that part of his life is finished. He returns to Sydney, Australia, where he enters into a masochistic relationship with a woman named Nance. He also begins to paint as he likes, rejecting "meaning" in the usual sense: "If you could put it in words," he tells his woman Nance, "I wouldn't want to paint it" (177). She does not understand, of course, as Hurtle confounds feeling and intellect in his intense perceptions. He still both *sees* and *feels* the chandelier "waiting in his mind and balls" (187). Mixing his paints with his lust, he has himself become a vivisector, one who would kill if necessary to explore interiors.

Nance tries vainly to expose Hurtle's myth about himself, but she is soon killed more or less accidentally by falling over the edge of a cliff. Hurtle is relieved although he feels some guilt over the fact that he probably could have prevented the accident.

Hurtle's first serious exhibit is criticized as pretentious. Shortly thereafter, a mysterious rich woman begins to purchase his work. When he discovers that his patroness is a childhood friend, the former Boo Hollingdrake, Hurtle begins an equivocal relationship with her, hallucinating Boo as one of his victims: "Here was another one, he saw, offering her throat to be cut, but by a more tortuous, a more jagged knife" (256).

Through Boo he eventually meets an enigmatic Greek woman, magnificently named Hero. When Hurtle calls God "The Divine Destroyer" (307), she is not shocked and they soon become lovers. Married to a millionaire, Hero offended her husband by her lustfulness. Now as Hurtle's mistress, her "Byzantine hunger" (324) attracts and repels him as he goes through "his trampoline act" (326). Hurtle tries to paint their lust as "an expression of truth, on that borderline where the hideous and depraved can become aesthetically acceptable" (329).

Hero takes her new lover to a beloved Greek island. She hopes "the devils may be cast out in the holy places of Perialos" (340), but the visit is a failure, and the affair ends with Hero justifying herself: "I do not understand the mind of an artist. He is too egoist, too enclosed" (356). Hurtle adjusts and goes home to live alone. As he grows older, his neighbors consider him "crazy as a cut snake. That's what art does for yer" (362).

After Hero's death, Hurtle again feels stirrings of guilt but in time he exorcises that ghost, too, and begins a relationship with a young musician, Kathy Volkov. He also invites his step-sister, Rhoda, now an old hag, to move in with him, but at first she is reluctant. "I might be vivisected afresh," she tells him, "in the name of truth—or art" (406). She explains: "I was born vivisected. I couldn't bear to be strapped to the table again" (407). Despite her doubts, however, Rhoda moves in, bringing fifteen cats with her.

Meanwhile, Hurtle paints furiously, including many likenesses of his new love, Kathy, at an old upright piano. When she wins a competition and must leave to further her career, Hurtle falls ill. He is frightened when he learns that Kathy's mother has had a "stroke" resulting in blurred speech. He massages his right hand anxiously: "So he lay wondering whether he believed in God the Merciful as well as God the Vivisector; he wondered whether he believed in God as he lay massaging his right hand" (448). For the time being, however, he survives to refuse a knighthood, while at home his life with Rhoda attains some stability. Hurtle continues to confound his secret paintings with his surrealistic anxiety dreams: "There was one drawing in which all the women he had ever loved were joined by umbilical cords to the navel of the same enormous child" (475).

After he breaks with Kathy and time passes, Hurtle realizes he is dying. Despite a paralyzed arm and a dragging leg, he has ordered many boards to be primed and arranged for a great painting. He has finally, as he always feared, been "stroked by God." He begins, nevertheless, to paint furiously: "Watching those daringly loose strokes of paint, which might have looked haphazard if they hadn't been compelled, he experienced a curious sense of grace" (564). He reaches for the ultimate color, indigo, and then, in a vision, as the syntax shatters and his sister prays, Hurtle dies. The last line of the book is enigmatic: "Too tired too endless obvi indi-ggoddd" (567) There is no period.

A Curious Sense of Grace

The novelist allows Hurtle to approach salvation when he writes that he "was suddenly carried, without choice, on the wings of his exhaustion, to the point of intellectual and—dare he begin to say it?—spiritual self-justification" (430). It seems, however, that White intended to leave Hurtle's redemption in doubt. One of the four epigraphs to the novel is from St. Augustine: "They love truth when it reveals itself, and they hate it when it reveals themselves." Readers were forewarned that they might find the truth in the novel anathema.

One critic took the bait: "From the opening paragraph—or more precisely from the title-page—all the cards are stacked against it. The Artist is a SYMBOL: and Patrick White can rarely if ever resist a really ham-fisted symbol, all meaty with meaning." Thus Richard Coe, an Australian critic, begins his scathing denunciation of *The Vivisector*. Coe rejects all the characters: "Platitudes, all of them. But leavened (since Patrick White is a fashionable artist) with fashionable tit-bits. Discretely-distributed four-letter words. Enlivening farts. At least two homosexuals. . . ."[5]

Others were more cautious. David Pryce-Jones penetrated the mystery: "Through Duffield we may see Mr. White."[6] Noting the first evidence of smut in White's prose, Patricia

Morley tried to reconstruct the *real* White behind the naughty façade, reasoning that White was justified: "Both man and his world are simultaneously 'shit and light' . . . or 'illuminated dust'. . . ."[7]

White's credentials were being investigated at this time, and it was rumored that the conservative Nobel Prize Committee was not pleased with this novel because it called God a vivisector. Such a simplification, however, is a misreading of the novel, for it is the artist who vivisects when he becomes God's surrogate as a creator. God-as-vivisector is only one side of the coin. The epigraph from Rimbaud points to the paradox that is at the heart of the novel: "He becomes beyond all others the great Invalid, the great Criminal, the great Accursed One—and the Supreme Knower. For he reaches the unknown." Significantly, the second "he" is not capitalized, dropping from the upper case of Invalid, Criminal, Accursed One, and Supreme Knower to lower case, suggesting that God as man can succeed in reaching the unknown. White, like Rimbaud, is not burdened with the need to rationalize Christian theology. He is not, however, a Satanist, as Rimbaud may have been. William Walsh, who is not compelled to filter out heresies in White's novel, makes peace with the work: "The real achievement of *The Vivisector* is the marvellous matching of considerable powers with a subject of exceptional difficulty, and the harmonious employment of both to develop a vision of human life in one of its most sensitive phases, which some may take to be cruel but which seems to me implacably accurate and just."[8]

The Eye of the Storm

Just as *The Vivisector* seems at times to speak in tongues, its sermons in *Dreck* distasteful to the faint-hearted, White's next novel, *The Eye of the Storm*, speaks in exotic ways, glorifying a selfish old lady, debasing her son and daughter into killers, and celebrating *Sturm* and *Drang* as leading to the peace that passes all understanding. Without a storm there can be no peaceful eye of the storm, although it is wise to remember that the eye predicts the return of the storm with the wind coming from the opposite direction. Thus there are two chances to be destroyed.

Elizabeth Hunter still remembers vividly the calm remission in the eye during a violent typhoon. In contrast, Mrs. Hunter's daughter, Dorothy de Lascambes, a princess by a marriage now shattered, has learned of such experiences only through others. Flying home from Europe to the bedside of her mother, she is frightened by the excessive turbulence. When she confesses her fear to the solid Dutchman sitting beside her, he tells her about his experience in a typhoon. He remembers particularly the peace and quiet of the eye:

Some years ago I was at sea—master of a freighter . . . when a typhoon struck us, almost fatally. For several hours we were thrown and battered—till suddenly calm fell—the calmest calm I have ever experienced at sea. God had willed us to enter the eye—you know about it? The still centre of the storm—where we lay at rest—surrounded by hundreds of seabirds, also resting on the water.[9]

Although Dorothy never sees the Dutchman again, she recalls him clearly as she tells her dying mother about the incident, describing him as "the soul of calm and wisdom" (72). Mrs. Hunter then relives her own experience as she reminisces to her daughter. Some years earlier the sixty-year-old widow and Dorothy accepted an invitation to share a primitive summer home on Brumby Island with Jack and Helen Warming. Helen Warming was a schoolmate of Dorothy's and at first Dorothy believes that her mother has been invited as a concession. She soon understands, however, that the Warmings adore Elizabeth. En route, Dorothy is further depressed by the physical attractiveness of the young pilot of the helicopter that their host had chartered for them. She tells herself that she despises "the law which decrees that almost everybody shall desire some other human being" (378).

Not long after her arrival Dorothy has a brief and sterile involvement with the Warmings' other house guest, a Norwegian professor. Leaving the island abruptly, she misses the great storm.

Mrs. Hunter, temporarily alone on the island, flees to the beach when the storm begins: "She was blown back no

longer any question of where twirled pummelled the um-
brella her dress pulled inside out over her head then returned
her breasts ribcage battered objects blood running from her
forehead she could feel taste thinned with water a salt rain"
(422).

Later she finds a shelter: "She lay and submitted to someone to whom she had never been introduced. Somebody is
always tinkering with something. It is the linesman testing
for the highest pitch of awfulness the human spirit can endure. Not death. For yourself there was no question of
dying" (423–24). When the storm abates as the eye
approaches, Mrs. Hunter leaves her shelter to embrace the
calm on the beach: In the eye "thousands of seabirds were at
rest; or the birds would rise, and dive, or peacefully scrabble
at the surface for food . . . " (424). She fed the wild swans
scraps of bread, which they accepted " . . . acknowledging
an equal" (425).

After the quiet interlude Mrs. Hunter awaits the return of
the storm in her bunker-shelter. She has had her "lustrous
moment made visible in the eye of the storm" although she
was not permitted to tarry there long. She soon returns,
however, to her everyday life, and in time grows old.

The Killing

Elizabeth Hunter's two children, Sir Basil and Dorothy, are
arranging the death of the old lady. Mrs. Hunter is to be
removed from her home when a vacancy occurs in a convenient nursing home. The children will supervise the removal,
allowing Mother a token selection of her own furniture. Mrs.
Hunter seems to agree but sardonically notes that a vacancy
should not be long in presenting itself: "They must be dying
all the time" (429).

Meanwhile, Basil and his sister decide to visit their childhood home, "Kudjeri," in the country nearby. The present
tenants agree to put up Basil and Dorothy for several days,
but the visit is heavy with sadness and spiced only by incestuous feelings between brother and sister, and by
Dorothy's disgust mixed with lust whenever she encounters
her host, the tenant farmer, Rory Macrory. Rory is physical
and smells of sweat.

During this interlude, which is a curt eye in the stormy lives of the siblings, the attention shifts to Basil, then back to Dorothy, as the two indulge themselves in the past. The pedestrian activities of the tenant family serve as norms against which the egoistic preoccupations of the siblings are measured. Macrory's animal insolence, heightened by alcohol, penetrates Dorothy's defenses and robs her of her customary rationalizations. On the last night of the visit she and her brother sleep together in their parents' old bed, which serves as "an island of frozen ridges and inky craters" (527).

Meanwhile, Elizabeth Hunter takes her time dying—at home, for she has decided that she will control the matter of her demise herself. The members of the affluent household and other attendants, such as Mrs. Hunter's solicitor, are woven into the story, including three nurses, a more-or-less faithful doctor, a devoted housekeeper, a part-time cleaning woman, and the solicitor's wife. Although Mrs. Hunter long ago committed intermittent adultery with her solicitor, by now his wife has become her uneasy confidante.

The three nurses appear in overlapping shifts. Their names suggest their roles at the allegorical level of the story. Sister de Santis is a fifteen-year veteran of the Hunter household. Senior to the others, she takes on her cases as spiritual proving grounds. Sister Badgery, true to her name, is a nag. She reminds Mrs. Hunter's solicitor Wyburd "of a white Leghorn: inquisitive, ostentatiously industrious, silly, easily outraged" (40). In contrast, Sister Manhood is a woman in bloom, possessed of skills useful to Mrs. Hunter. For example, she paints Mrs. Hunter's withered cheeks, adorns the balding head with a lavender wig, and fits the withered mouth with false teeth.

The housekeeper, Lotte Lippman, was once an entertainer in Germany. As a Jew, she suffered much guilt over her love for a German gentile. She knows Mrs. Hunter is selfish and cruel, but because Lotte is, as Mrs. Hunter once informed her, "the original masochist," she is able truly to love the old lady. "And," she shrewdly tells Sir Basil, "if I cannot worship, I have to love somebody" (150).

Sir Basil becomes involved with two of the nurses in interludes that establish him as a tepid villain. First Sister

Manhood seduces Basil, hoping that he will impregnate her so that she may have a child by her "master." She does not, however, succeed in her ultimate purpose. This affair, with its dark religious overtones, is contrasted with an ingenuous relationship between Basil and Sister de Santis when her concern for her patient leads her to a rendezvous at the seashore with Basil, ostensibly to plead for the life of Elizabeth Hunter. When the corpse of a dog is suddenly washed up on the sand before them, the stench offends Basil but is quietly accepted by Sister de Santis, who notices that the dog has been strangled with a wire around his neck.

As James Joyce once insisted, "dog" is "god" spelled backwards. A kind of mock-litany now takes over. Sister de Santis stumbles and falls as she is getting out of Basil's car when he returns her to the Hunter residence and to her duty. Wounded and bleeding, Sister de Santis refuses help from Basil. Contrite, he ends the night alone scribbling at a play, with the impending "murder" of his mother on his conscience.

Mrs. Hunter does not die before Lotte Lippman dances for her a resurrection of one of Lotte's long-ago performances as an entertainer. The scene accelerates into mad ecstasy as the dance begins to possess Lotte. Mrs. Hunter first fights against, then yields to her identification with the dancer. She also remembers an old dying cow she once came across when she was a girl. Other allusions previously established reappear, including the wild horses on Brumby Island. Mrs. Hunter finally dismisses Lotte, calls for Sister Manhood to help her onto the commode. There, seated on her "throne," she dies.

To add to the horror of the final scene, Mrs. Hunter is betrayed by her makeup artist, Sister Manhood. Preparing for Lotte's dance, Mrs. Hunter asked to be repristinated. Sister Manhood yields to the temptation to do "a real hatchet job for once" (539). Consequently, when she dies, Mrs. Hunter's face is painted in "shimmering greens of all fiends; the idol's brutal mouth . . . with a thick wall of black . . . " (539–40).

The curtain then falls, with a difference, on each of the characters—with irony or wisdom or peace or squalor. Lotte kills herself in the bath. Others adjust, cynically or desperately. Mrs. Hunter's solicitor steals a jewel he fancies. Daughter Dorothy returns to France, richer in money but poorer for having never experienced the eye of the storm. Sister Badgery embarks on a coach tour of New Zealand. Sir Basil flies off to Amsterdam.

Finally, Sister de Santis picks the last rose in Mrs. Hunter's garden. The rose will become her first gift to her new patient, waiting for a grace the patient has not earned but will receive freely from Sister de Santis.

A Little Crooked

Peter Beatson believes that both Hurtle and Elizabeth Hunter as well as Voss are intended to be "granted Grace." He does, however, add that they are not really "Great Criminals and Great Invalids"—categories challenging God, presumably, to show His Omnipotent Graciousness. Beatson admits that both Hurtle and Elizabeth are "a little crooked." As for Voss, he is "more than a little sick." Among the *illuminati*, the trio are involved in "a more bitter and protracted contest with God." Beatson, of course, believes that suffering is redemptive: "At the lowest point of the descent, when he has arrived at Calvary, man merges with God."[10] There is no real evidence, however, that White was that theological when he put Elizabeth Hunter through her suffering, some of which she enjoyed—especially when it made others unhappy.

In contrast to Beatson, George Steiner rises to heights of eloquence as he blasts the novel: "There is, in fact, not a touch of redeeming elegance, of disinterested humanity in 'The Eye of the Storm.' Everything tilts to ugliness or lumbering ferocity."[11] In the same vein, the anonymous critic in the *Times* (London) notes how he was turned off by the "hatred, disgust, and dislike," which is "excessive and hence fatally detrimental to what should have been a great novel."[12]

The novel is another happy hunting ground for ambitious critics. For example, Mrs. Hunter has been compared to Shakespeare's King Lear. Also the influence of the paintings of Paul Klee and stylized Noh dramas upon the imagery and action in the novel has been evaluated. [13] Not least, of course, is the certain influence of the novelist's mother on his portrait of Mrs. Hunter, an influence which makes loftier analogs seem somewhat ridiculous. In the end, Mrs. Hunter remains a selfish old lady, unredeemed and grotesque.

Chapter Seven
Epiphanies in Tables and Goats: *The Burnt Ones, The Cockatoos,* and *Four Plays*

Most of Patrick White's short stories have been collected and published in two volumes, *The Burnt Ones* (1964) and *The Cockatoos* (1975). Four of his early plays, originally produced in Australia, have been published in one volume in 1965. For many admirers of Patrick White, his shorter fiction and his plays are epiphenomena. That is, although White's reputation as a significant writer may be reinforced by them, they are not essential. Like his novels, they do, however, bear witness to the author's cosmopolitanism and his ambivalence about Australia. The stories in particular, which vary in length from extended sketches to novellas, employ diverse techniques for a wide range of effects.

When White returned to Australia after years abroad as a student, a soldier, and a wanderer, he brought with him memories of his sojourns in exotic places, material which he used in his short fiction. He was unsympathetic with the Australian literary nationalism that had emerged during the 1930s.[1] The writings of Joseph Furphy and Henry Lawson were always cited as examples of what the home folks could do. Both Furphy and Lawson were masters of the anecdotal style and their stories are easy to understand. Their home-spun quality contrasts with the literary sophistication of White and Richardson, who could not conceal, even if they had chosen, their interest in the experiments of British and Continental dramatists and storytellers.

Patriots such as Nettie Palmer continued to prefer the home-made stories of Henry Lawson, for example, praising their "loose, easy look."[2] At the same time, others began to break away from the old ways. Hal Porter, for one, took a new look at familiar places and people. G. A. Wilkes was one of the critics who understood what Porter was trying to do, and he tried to explain it: "The world of Porter's stories is the familiar world seen as slightly askew, the personalities sometimes neurotic, the events sometimes macabre." Human beings are perceived as "enigmatic and astonishing."[3] Just as Virginia Woolf in England had rejected giglamps for the personal reality of luminous halos, Christina Stead and Randolph Stow in Australia—as well as White and Porter—began to express impressions rather than report. White's short stories, in particular, led the way.

The Burnt Ones

Patrick White's first collection, which he called *The Burnt Ones*, contains eleven stories. Nine of them originally appeared in periodicals such as *Meanjin, Australian Letters,* and *London Magazine.*[4] Several of the stories are Greek in setting and characters. One mixes modalities by transporting an Australian woman to Greece for its moment of truth. One is set in the neutral city of Geneva, while others are highlighted by the plastic suburbia near Sydney which White calls Sarsaparilla. All of them, however, investigate concerns familiar to White's readers: suffering, loneliness, and frustration as constants in the human equation, an equation in which the variables may contain humor and irony but seldom high tragedy.

White found ideas and characters compatible with his themes—unfortunates burned by life—while living in postwar Greece where he met and sympathized with the victims and exiles whose quest for salvation had been secularized by wartime hardships. God seemed remote and improbable, often even a mockery after the "Catastrophe" at Smyrna, where many Greeks were slaughtered by the Turks and others fled with their lives only. Also, severe shortages following World War II, particularly in Athens, where aristocrats were forced to forage for food, intensified passions and escalated issues.

In "The Woman who wasn't Allowed to Keep Cats" White contrasts two rich, Americanized Greeks, proud owners of a Cadillac, with a married couple struggling to adjust to life in Athens. The local Greeks seem eccentric. The man is a left-wing writer, the woman a cat-lover. The "authentic" Greek woman blames her compatriots for not loving cats. Greeks, she says, are "too egotistical, quarrelsome, lazy, and gluttonous to understand the force of love" (257). The visitors find the cat-lover mad, and when they return two years later to visit their friends again, they discover that the cat-lover has given up her cats because the formerly liberal husband has forbidden them now that he is a prosperous, right-wing writer. The Americanized Greeks get the impression that the cat-lover has been transformed into a cat. They are glad to return to New York. No one has escaped deterioration.

In another of the Greek stories, "The Evening at Sissy Kamara's," memories of Smyrna are the pedal point in a contrapuntal conversation between two couples. The hostess, Sissy, once had intellectual pretensions. She has published some poems, but "so privately nobody has read them." Once she declaimed an epic poem—"On a theme nobody can remember," says Basil Patzopoulos upon being informed by Poppy, his wife, that she has accepted an invitation to spend an evening at Sissy's. Of Sissy's declamation he adds: "On a mountain side. To a group of women, most of them by now dead" (128–29).

In the course of the evening the hosts and guests share a small balcony. As Sissy serves indifferent food, her husband breaks Sissy's last good dish from Smyrna. In a confusion of emotions Sissy laughs as she cries, then philosophizes: "Almost my last possession of importance . . . when one had hoped with age to grow less attached when age itself is the arch-disappointer a final orgy of possessiveness of of of [*sic*] a gathering of minor vanities" (139). Sissy also "explains" Greeks to her guests: "We are a brutal, detestable race," she pontificates. "If we care to admit, we are little better than Turks turned back to front" (136). Although Basil and Poppy Patzopoulos disagree with Sissy, they suppress possible rejoinders and depart with feelings of guilt. There is no resolution.

"Being Kind to Titina" begins in Alexandria where a "good" Greek family and a "bad" Greek family are neighbors; then the story moves on to Athens for an ironic conclusion. There the Greek boy-man from the good family has his first sexual experience with an amoral but happy whore. The woman turns out to be the formerly plain Titina from the bad Greek family, whom he had once been forced to treat politely when they were childhood neighbors. The upgrading of Titina is contrasted with the disillusionment of the good boy. Again, however, there is no resolution.

In "A Glass of Tea" White utilizes Geneva as a neutral setting for a conversation between two casual acquaintances, both Greeks of different histories and generations. Malliakas, a middle-aged bachelor, a writer manqué in search of a story and in Geneva on business, finally decides to present a letter of introduction to Philippides, an elderly Greek now living in Switzerland. During his short visit Malliakas finds his story. It is based on what the old man tells him of his first wife, Constantia, emended by what the old man's second wife, Aglaia, tells him about the first wife and a set of tea glasses. A gypsy had once prophesied that the old man would live until the last of the glasses was broken, but it was his first wife who broke instead. At the time of the visit there is just one glass left unbroken. It will not last long, however, Malliakas knows, as he sadly leaves.

In "Dead Roses" White combines the decadence of Greece with the sterility of respectable Australia. Anthea Scudmore, a forerunner of Theodora Goodman of *The Aunt's Story*, is a wealthy Australian widow traveling in Greece. There she is eventually rebuffed by a former admirer also visiting Greece. She is also insulted and threatened by a beautiful young Athenian. That night the Australian woman, who is so sterile that most flowers die on her, dreams neither of the young Greek nor of her former admirer but rather of the latter's wife, who had been wearing "stained leopard-skin matador pants" (66). The story is heavy with Freudian symbols and itself ends in a dying fall—as dead as the dead roses Anthea had found in the home of her impotent husband on her wedding night.

The Australian stories in the collection often satirize generalizations that begin "We Australians," but with a difference from the "We Greeks" philosophers. There is less poignancy in the Australians, with whom White is less patient than he is with babbling Greeks. In "Miss Slattery and her Demon Lover" an Australian lady objects strenuously when she hears her country reduced to "nossing" by her Hungarian lover. She counters at once with "we Australians are not all that uncivilized. Not in 1961" (200). Miss Slattery, however, is not taken very seriously by Tibby Szabo, her masochistic, rich, and fat Hungarian lover, until she threatens to leave him. When Szabo asks her if she is "ze Defel perheps?" she answers: "We Australians are not all that unnatural" (215).

In "A Cheery Soul" a self-righteous husband and wife argue themselves into sharing their home with an unfortunate woman, a Miss Docker. When the arrangement soon turns into a domestic disaster, the "cheery soul" is transferred to a respectable institution for impecunious aged men and women. There her cheeriness moves from nuisance to menace when she challenges the minister in church, destroying his sermon and literally striking him down so that the minister's wife accuses her of having killed not only her husband but perhaps also her God. The effect of such blasphemy is devastating, as White well knew, and he later developed this story into a drama.

Reasonable people often insist on being considered both civilized and normal and are easily satirized because no one is ever quite reasonable except in his own opinion. When the hero of the story "Clay" asks his mother why she named him Clay, he receives a reasonable answer: his mother had been interested in making pottery. There is little else in the sketch, but it makes a sharp point economically. In another short piece, "The Letters," a mother-dominated son finally tries to make love to his mother. White suggests that the son's violent behavior was programmed by his mother's devotion to him. The incest episode yields to an anticlimax. Instructed as a child never to read other people's letters, the son finally stops reading even those addressed to him!

In the most ambitious story in the collection, "Down at the Dump," a boy-man and girl-woman meet at the line be-

tween the dump and the cemetery, having been brought to
the dump and the cemetery respectively by their parents.
The boy's family are "doing the dump"—which means
scavenging. The girl's parents are burying a relative, Daise, a
woman of easy virtue. It is clear that she is also one of the *illuminati* when at the cemetery her spirit speaks of love.

Although the meeting between the youths is contrived, the
effect crescendoes before the quiet ending as the potential
lovers return home with their respective parents, passing
one another on the road: "They lowered their eyes, as if
they had seen enough for the present, and wished to cherish
what they knew" (308).

Big questions are asked of Destiny and Accident in the
story called "Willy-Wagtails by Moonlight" via a slip in the
making of a tape of the song of a bird. A respectable husband, while recording the Willy-Wagtail, also inadvertently
records the sounds of his adultery with his secretary. Only a
visiting couple, however, hear that part of the tape, the unfaithful husband and the betrayed wife being destined accidentally to be out of the room. This trivial and bitter story is
characteristic of the "black in White." Accidents are the
only miracles.

The Cockatoos

The Cockatoos, White's second collection of stories, appeared in 1975.[5] It contains six substantial pieces of short
fiction which testify to the writer's growing maturity. Less
gimmicky than several of the stories in *The Burnt Ones*,
these later narratives reflect the author's concern for ways in
which desperate human beings confront the odds against
them. Here a few of them are allowed to find a kind of salvation outside churches, or even in the improper use of a
church as a place of assignation. White's secular offerings include a cup of coffee, a handful of rice, a glimpse of cockatoos or peacocks, sunsets, and an old man's urine.

In "The Night the Prowler" an old man, far into his dying,
explains to a young woman that there are only two goods: to
piss easily and to shit smoothly. And so when he urinates
over himself as the woman holds his hand, the woman feels a
momentary grace as "she continued up the hill to report the

death of an old man she had discovered a few moments before, but knew as intimately as she knew herself, in solitariness, in desolation, as well as in what would seem to be the dizzy course of perpetual becoming" (168).

Evelyn Bannister, the recipient of this unusual grace, is just nineteen years old on the eventful night in which she encounters a prowler in her home. The assumption that she is raped and otherwise mistreated by the prowler is the invention of her parents and neighbors, who need to be protected from the truth that Evelyn frightens the prowler more than he frightens her. After drinking and smoking in his presence, she sends him away, disgusted by his unimaginative timidity.

Soon thereafter, using her "rape" as an excuse, Evelyn cancels her engagement to a nice young man, who is relieved. Evelyn then begins to break into houses in the neighborhood herself, not to steal or rape but to extend her freedom. In the final, good-Samaritan scene she embraces a repulsive derelict. He dies in her arms while offering her his urine.

In "Sicilian Vespers" White again challenges convention and Christian morality. The piece is a carefully dramatized tale about a failure of faith between persons who rely too heavily on rationalism and humanism. Ivy and Charles Simpson represent those Australians who accept being Australian without either glorifying colonialism or hating other colonials, such as Americans. The Simpsons are genuinely kind, honest, intelligent, and well enough off to travel. Abroad, they tolerate foreign eccentricities they would not dream of accepting at home. In Sicily their planned itinerary becomes an empty time because of Charles's almost incapacitating toothache.

During the pause the Simpsons make friends with the Clark Shacklocks, a rich American couple who seem a bit vulgar but kind. Clark *may* be Roman Catholic but the Simpsons are not sure. His wife Imelda certainly seems to be a Christian Scientist. As the relationship between the couples begins to get complicated, Ivy Simpson suddenly, against her better judgment, allows herself to be possessed one evening by Clark in the Duomo at San Fabrizio during vespers. Imelda and Charles, meanwhile, wait patiently for their respective spouses in the lobby of the hotel. Imelda is reading an ironically appropriate Italian novel: *I Promessi Sposi*.

Upon her return, Ivy Simpson remains cool and lies. She later realizes she is still hungry for a religious experience, or rather, she tells herself, at least for religious words. She had always respected the word "*Godhead*: as a mere word leaping at her from off the printed page, it made her turn over quickly, to escape something far beyond what Charles and she had agreed to find acceptable" (230).

In "A Woman's Hand" Clem Dowson tries to explain to his friend, Harold Fazackerly, why he and his wife have separated:

"My God," Dowson was gasping and mouthing, "one day, Harold, when we meet—in different circumstances—I must try to tell you all I've experienced." He was speaking from behind closed eyes. "That was the trouble between us. Between myself and that woman. We had lived at the same level. It was too great a shock to discover there was someone who could read your thoughts." (76)

There is no chance, however, for the two men to meet "in different circumstances," for that night Clem is killed by a bus whose wheels he makes no attempt to avoid. Harold is left friendless and confused, realizing he has missed something. His need, however, has not been defined so there is no way of satisfying it. Also, Harold's wife, despite her good intentions, cannot understand either her husband's need or that of his friend. It was she who was originally responsible for adding "a woman's hand" to bachelor Clem's house overlooking the sea. The woman she paired with Clem, however, ends in a psychiatric hospital: she had heard the sunset shriek "with the throats of peacocks" (70). The moral is a bitter one: it is dangerous to hear the sunset shriek.

In the title story of the collection, "The Cockatoos," a Mrs. Davoren and her husband are as alienated from one another as possible until the cockatoos arrive. They have not exchanged spoken words for years. When necessary, they communicate via pencil and pad. But when they see the spectacular cockatoos, the Davorens begin to speak to one another again—about the birds, of course—and even celebrate their reunion in bed. Their joy is short-lived, however. One day a neighbor shoots two of the birds, and in the ensuing struggle for the gun Mr. Davoren is killed. But that is not all that happens. When a neighbor boy, Tim Goodenough, finds the last of the cockatoos, a cripple, he kills it and cuts off the bird's crest as a trophy to mark his victory. Cockatoos can bring joy to those who love them but the price is high.

The two most ambitious stories in the collection are "Five-Twenty" and "The Full Belly," each of which celebrates a secular communion and its terrifying inadequacy: a cup of coffee that is never served and a handful of rice that degrades decent people. In the former story a childless, elderly couple spend their days sitting on a porch watching the traffic pass on the highway. Royal and Ellen Natwick are dependent on the regularity in the lives of others, particularly upon a man in a Holden who drives by at five-twenty every evening. He is a flat-headed, unusual looking fellow. They have found him memorable and essential. If he occasionally misses his "five-twenty" passing, the Natwicks are upset. Their clock has betrayed them: the universe is not orderly after all.

When Royal Natwick dies quietly, Ella is left "with his hand, already set, in her own. They hadn't spoken except about whether she had put out the garbage" (184). Ella accepts widowhood and takes the pills the doctor prescribes. As far as she can, she begins to relate to her "things," among which the man in the Holden is still real. Then one day he stops and asks to use the phone.

Excited, unable to speak clearly, she babbles in a "new language." He is not upset. He holds her in his arms. She responds, watching "the world of his mouth"—he has a hare lip—"struggling to open." At this moment of recognition Ella kisses him "as though she might never succeed in healing all the wounds they had ever suffered" (190). He promises to return the next day for a cup of coffee. In the meantime Ella learns how to make coffee, having had previous experience with tea only. This communion cup will contain a brew new to her.

When five-twenty comes and passes without him, Ella fears the worst. There is a bad wreck up the road. Has he perhaps been killed? He finally appears: he is late because he is ill. The symptoms indicate angina, with pains up and down his left arm. Ella vows to save him. In fact, however, in her eagerness she embraces him too forcefully and kills him "by loving too deep, and too adulterously" (196). The author's verdict is ruthless: Ella's worldly reward for all that patient watching was only a chance at adultery, no more and no less than a chance, and she lost. The coffee was never served.

The rice becomes moot in the story "The Full Belly," which returns to the Athenian scene. During the occupation of Greece, Athenians were severely tested not only by hunger but also by a patriotism that required strict resistance to collaboration. Two proud and elderly spinster sisters, Maro and Pronoë, have long ago bartered away all their valuable possessions for food but still refuse to collaborate with the prosperous Germans who occupy the city. The older sister, Maro, begins to starve herself to death in order to save food for others in the family. Her nephew, Costa, who is a talented music student and the orphaned son of a former President of Greece, decides to sell himself for food.

Costa first refuses the advances of a neighbor woman who would pay him in eggs. He then encounters a German soldier in one of the side streets of Athens who offers him meat in exchange for what Costa knows he has already done but this time chooses to refuse. Not much later, driven by hunger for meat, he changes his mind and searches for the soldier, who, however, has disappeared. Rushing home because he remembers a dish of rice left next to dying Aunt Maro's bedside, he finds Aunt Pronoë already there and gorging herself on the few grains of rice. They struggle for the food, breaking the dish in the contest. After Pronoë leaves in disgust, Costa kneels and picks up bits of rice mixed with bits of carpet and stuffs them into his mouth. When his dying aunt sees him, she says: "Eat, poor souls. . . . Fill your stomachs, children." Then she adds, before she dies: "I only pray you'll know how to forgive each other" (118). After such knowledge, what forgiveness?

Secular Sacraments

The extent to which one can accept White's specifications for and significance of the "course of perpetual becoming," which for him is obviously a good—if not the only good—in living, correlates with the degrees of praise allowed these stories. The alleged epiphanies are often blurred. Grace is neither easily won nor freely bestowed by either writer or reader. Characters behaving decently in a godless universe are sometimes seen as foolish. What price courage if there is no reward here or in an afterlife? Certainly White allows little probability of judgment days that will rectify and punish fairly.

The Cockatoos is condemned as "a strong anti-marriage tract" by a woman obviously upset about the failure of marital bonds in the stories to restrain immorality. The same critic prefers White's novels, concluding that "the short story does not offer White the space he needs for his greatest strength, the portrayal of a character's fantasy."[6] Eudora Welty, however, praises White's stories, noting that "they go off like cannons fired over some popular, scenic river—depth charges to bring up the drowned bodies."[7] Brian Kiernan compares White's stories favorably with those of Hal Porter, finding that "White's style has become more muted over the years, more an instrument than a self-regarding end." Unlike Porter, however, "White is concerned to engage life, and in the better stories, this takes the form of his emphatically imagining how life might be experienced by others."[8]

White's shorter fiction has recently been honored by a book-length study in which David Myers explores the many "dualities" in the stories: " . . . not only the tragic irreconcilability of such antitheses as grace and horror, epiphany and sanity, caritative love and bourgeois conventions. . . . There is also the dual vision of his irony which incessantly modifies both the bitterness and the bliss of his protagonists." Because there is less room to manipulate these dualities in a short story, the pieces are not all equally successful. Furthermore, what Myers calls "White's grotesque sense of

humour" seems harsher in the short stories, and Myers notes
that White has confessed that he does not like writing
shorter fiction as much as he does a novel. "All my effects
are cumulative," White has said, "and one doesn't really
have the time to get the effects you want."[9]

Four Plays

White's earliest experiments with drama did not find their
way into a collection, although there is evidence that they,
too, were attempts to engage life.[10] He had early rejected
"backyard realism," as Hugh Hunt called the trend before
1960 in the Australian theater.[11] *The Ham Funeral* was written in the middle 1940s but not produced until 1961. Even
then it was too advanced for its time. When it was finally
produced by the Adelaide University Theatre Guild in
association with the Elizabethan Theatre Trust, it became
something of a celebrated cause. At the time White said that
he would never write another play. He was, however,
already at work on *The Season at Sarsaparilla*, which
was soon followed by *A Cheery Soul* and *Night on Bald
Mountain*.

Actually White had little competition in Australia in his
role as rebel in the theater. Modern Australian drama did not
really begin until Ray Lawler's *The Summer of the Seven-
teenth Doll* was produced in 1955, a play which, according
to G. A. Wilkes "was so 'Australian' . . . that it was to prove
a revelation to audiences in London . . . New York . . . even
Iceland—while at home it suggested that the self-discovery
that had occurred in the other fields in the 1890s had now
come about in the native drama."[12] *The Doll* tells the story of
two mates and their women against the background of the
great outdoors. It is Australian in idiom and values and is
noteworthy today only for its historical significance, an-
nouncing as it did outside Australia that the colony was not
entirely illiterate.

White's adventures as a playwright in the 1960s were still
controversial. *The Ham Funeral* is discussed above in
Chapter 2 as a part of his apprentice work. The three later
dramas are more nearly typical of the mature writer's concerns and idiom. In *The Season at Sarsaparilla, A Cheery*

Soul, and *Night on Bald Mountain* failed saints and second-rate devils debate big issues in modest ways. Attention to realistic detail competes with transcendent imagery. Little things have big implications. For example, when the dogs begin to bark in Sarsaparilla, everyone understands that the "season" has come around again. Not only is the local bitch in heat, but also the humans are restless. Something is bound to happen in town.

Sarsaparilla and Its Ways

The Season at Sarsaparilla locates three families on stage via "boxes," each one the kitchen area of a house. The basic units of the cast are three married couples. Variety is added to the basics by introducing a bachelor brother of one wife, a woman friend of one daughter, a girl friend of one child, two suitors of the eligible daughter, a fiancée of a friend, and the mate of one husband. The mate spends two nights with his friend and his friend's wife, the first on the sofa, the second in the bed of his friend's wife. This quick adultery is made possible by the fact that the cuckolded husband works nights as a "sanitary man." Other events appropriate to suburbia occur in the course of the play.

Fornication among the dogs in Sarsaparilla is confined to once every six months and to the one bitch in heat and as many male animals as the bitch will service. Among the humans it is not that simple. Lust both frustrates and accelerates human sex behavior, which is always in season. In the course of this play there is one pregnancy, unwanted and eventually the cause of a suicide, one legitimate birth, and assorted, tepid caresses of habituated spouses dutifully performing Sarsaparilla rituals. Freedom is at a premium and quite risky in Sarsaparilla. Bondage is normal. Dreams of freedom identify the young, the insane, and the occasional hero. Penalties for either heroic or outrageous success are severe. The median is the mean. Deviation and skewed distribution are discouraged.

At the end of the play the heroic rebel in quest of his freedom leaves town. Looking back in sadness rather than anger at his neighbors as he is leaving, he says: "Listen to them, the poor sods! They'll still be at it when I get back. . . .

(*Slower, more thoughtful*) Because . . . of course . . . I *shall* get back. (*Exasperated*) You can't shed your skin . . . even if it itches like hell!'' (176–77).

Philanthropy in Sarsaparilla is as sad and equivocal as sexual love. In *A Cheery Soul* an apparently nice lady is both the giver and recipient of charity. Disaster is inevitable, for good intentions are the original irony in Creation. White called his original short story "A Cheery Soul" with gentle malice aforethought. The extended dramatic version intensifies the malice as several episodes are opened out. Miss Docker, the cheery soul of both story and play, is indeed a cheerful killer, first symbolically when she slaughters dreams and illusions of the less cheery people around her who try to be kind, and then literally when she challenges the minister's rhetoric in church.

The well-meaning clergyman has become entangled in his metaphor of the "ordinary pumpkin," which, he says, can be saved from "mildew and blight." Miss Docker answers: "Spray and pray! It is prayer that saves pumpkins. . . ." Meanwhile, the minister's wife prays for her poor husband: "Lord, show him . . . that pumpkins light lamps of splendour perched on iron roofs" (259). The wife's prayer is in vain, however, for Miss Docker persists in defending her own concept of sin, which, she says, "is what you make it. Or *un*-make" (259).

The minister's rational approach finally cracks when Miss Docker insists that "failure is not failure if it is sent to humble." Whereupon the minister, falling to his knees, cries out that he is "blinded" rather than "illuminated" (260). He collapses as his wife accuses Miss Docker of killing not only the minister but also her God.

In the end Miss Docker is rejected by a dog in the street, who pees on her leg as she realizes, appalled, that dog is God spelled backwards. And so, as Patrick White has his sport with mortals, Miss Docker sighs and decides to make the best of it: "I was never one to cry," she says. "Never ever . . . " (264).

The fourth play in the collection is the most rigorously patterned. In *Night on Bald Mountain* White gives the insight of a Rider in the Chariot to an old lady and fractions of that same vision to an alcoholic wife—at least when she is drunk—and to a nurse, who sees too much too soon to survive.

From the beginning it is clear that Miss Quodling is one of the *illuminati*. She lives on Bald Mountain with her goats, which is far from alone considering how she feels about goats. One of "the burnt ones," she has survived to find peace without losing the ability to share that peace with others. It is Miss Quodling who gives shelter to the frightened and ailing alcoholic, Mrs. Sword, on the climactic night on Bald Mountain. Mrs. Sword's nurse, Sister Summerhayes, has been forced to flee from her own incestuous desires, which have been cruelly identified for her by her employer, Professor Sword.

Sword, as his name shouts, is sharp and cuts. He is an intellectual; he is also clever, cruel, and a killer although providence also plays a part in the action, providing coincidences, accidents, and a mist on the mountain. When Sister Summerhayes—a nice name for a gentle woman who loves the sun and will die in a mist—goes over the cliff at the end, her death could conceivably have been an accident. Sword, however, takes the credit, accusing himself of forcing her to kill herself, for it was he who told her she desired her own father. For a moment or two he resolves to make some attempt to stop the systematic destruction of his wife, and the play ends before another killing.

Involved in all this are a stock housekeeper and an equally stock poetic young man, the professor's student, who is attracted to Mrs. Sword's nurse but who fumbles his sex plays and romantic ploys and symbolically becomes another one of Sword's victims. In the end Sword presumes to take credit for being sick, the only virtue left to a failed saint. Miss Quodling, however, endures, surviving even the death of her most beloved goat, who that night also falls over the cliff. Not surprisingly, the goat woman has the last words in the play: "There is no such thing as *nothun*! (*Softer*) The silence will breed again . . . in a world of goats . . . perhaps even men" (356).

A Passion for the Stage, But . . .

Most critics show respect for White's experimental dramas, noting that the writer certainly has a passion for the stage. The qualifications in the form of various "buts" that

often follow this acknowledgment are essentially praise for
his novels as superior pieces of literature. J. R. Dyce has
analyzed the four plays published in 1965 and has written a
book-length study which summarizes contemporary reactions to the live productions. Dyce stresses the controversial
aspects of White as a dramatist. Even before *The Ham
Funeral* was produced in 1961, the controversy was strong
enough to block its being presented at the Adelaide Festival
of Arts. It and two later plays were staged by the Adelaide
University Theatre Guild and inevitably viewed as "little
theater" and treated somewhat condescendingly, much as
an off-Broadway production in New York is expected to be
special—either very intellectual or very experimental but not
in the main stream. Later reactions to White's five serious
dramas—*Big Toys*, produced in 1977 is discussed below in
Chapter 8—assess them as literature; that is, they are read
rather than viewed, so that the printed words are not forced
to carry the same responsibility as spoken words which are
heard only once. It is, of course, not possible to re-read a
page, or even to pause, while experiencing a live play.

According to Dyce, critics ask the following questions of
White's plays: "Are they solid enough in construction to
weather the process of change, irrespective of their non-
naturalistic form which caused so much comment at first?
Has Patrick White's particular vitality as a novelist proved
too much for the genre he has chosen? Is he too demanding
as a playwright?"[13]

The answers vary. William Walsh feels that "all the plays
suggest a certain lack of confidence on the part of the
dramatist in his actors and partners." The dramatist appears
to be "ordering each step and shade in the action."[14] Walsh's
comments point toward the verdict that as a dramatist White
is more of a novelist. In this context, an American reviewer
said of *Four Plays*: "Good dialogue has always been a
feature of Patrick White's novels . . . and in these plays it
stands up on its own, so to speak. It stands up very well."[15]

A successful drama is, however, much more than good
dialogue. A novel (or a *printed* play) can be paced by the
reader, thus allowing the author to elaborate on subtle ideas
as well as aesthetic nuances that dull readers may take more

time to perceive. Also, a play does not accommodate shifting points of view nor can a dramatist usually comment on his own play while it is in action. White's obsession with symbols and images makes heavy demands on a theater audience. All in all White's passion for the theater has paid respectable dividends. His dramas—for his Australian audiences, at least—had the integrity of honest pioneering. The four plays produced in the 1960s were genuine voices in a theatrical wilderness. Later experiments in drama, including his own 1977 *Big Toys*, were viewed by Australian audiences that White had helped educate. No one, however, has seriously suggested that the literary world was significantly changed or even enhanced by White's plays as it has been by his novels. White's most impressive novels are possibly unique contributions to literature. They will certainly survive longer than his plays.

Chapter Eight
Patrick White Agonistes: *A Fringe of Leaves, Big Toys,* and *The Twyborn Affair*

In 1973 White admitted that "everything I write has to be dredged up from the unconscious—which is what makes it such an exhausting and perhaps finally, destructive, process. . . . My first draft of a novel is the work of intuition, and it is a chaos nobody but myself could resolve."[1] By then White had begun to weary of the esoteric explications of his novels in which almost every image and artifact must mean more than it seems at first. Although White pleased in-depth critics when he referred to his unconscious, he did not encourage zealous symbol-hunting: "This awful symbol business! . . . In their pursuit of symbols many academic critics can't seem to realize that writers and painters often make use of images and situations from real life because they have appealed to them as being beautiful or comic or bizarre. . . ." White also objected to "those indefatigable unravellers" who make too much of "colours." He asked: "Can't we use a colour because it *is*, or because we happen to like it? If purple crops up under the mulberry tree, aren't mulberries purple?"[2]

Once established as a prize-winner, the post-Nobel White was even more impatient with "academic vultures." Although a writer is not always a trustworthy witness to his own creative activities, especially if he is a master ironist, White's two novels and one play that followed his becoming a celebrity testify to his sincerity. His feeling that writing is an exhausting process is shared by most professionals but his feeling that it may also be destructive is part of White's own idiom and commitment. Both *A Fringe of Leaves* (1976) and *The Twyborn Affair* (1979), as well as his recent play, *Big Toys* (1977), are permeated with black humor and white agony as the writer reaches for ultimates.

White's commitment to tell the truth as he sees it entails scrupulous analyses of the limitations of free will as well as explorations of those accidents usually excused as acts of God. Sin is strictly a function of free will, and the guilt that follows sinful behavior is thus greater or lesser depending upon how free the sinner really is. Old theological dogmas have been yielding to psychological ones, in which sin is lessened by defining accidents as neither God's nor man's fault, and in which guilt is called anxiety and treated rather than punished. Nevertheless, terror and violence persist. Lightning strikes, floods occur, and epidemics spread.

White's *illuminati* have learned to distrust the platitudes that try to minimize the responsibility which God or providence or fate or destiny should morally assume. As they resist strokes and accidents they begin to act in self-defense. They become antagonists of God, and the story is the account of how they succeed or fail in outwitting the odds against them.

A Fringe of Leaves

Patrick White's use of accidents is never casual. He knows that a shipwreck, for example, is a perfect device for accidentally stranding one or more persons in a limited space where issues are perforce intensified. Shipwrecks, unlike plane crashes, often leave survivors about whom to weave a story. In the 1830s, the time of the action of White's *A Fringe of Leaves*, people traveled across oceans and even around the world in sailing ships, vessels vulnerable to meteorological events, which, for better or worse, were allegedly under the control of God. Thus a storm at sea challenged the traveler's faith, especially when the power plant which the traveler depended upon was God's wind striking man's sail. Danger at sea, such as a storm, stimulates both prayer and blasphemy. When a frightened person is forced to pray to God for protection against the acts of the same God, irony is the only refuge of the intelligent.

When the passengers on the brig, *Bristol Maid*, are forced to abandon ship after the vessel founders on a reef and the wind has struck down the main mast and shredded the sails, they have certainly experienced at its existentially fullest what it means to put oneself in the hands of God. Only a rare person could exult in such disorientation. White's Mrs. Roxburgh is such a person.[3] Born Ellen Gluyas in Cornwall, she has dreamed as a girl of a king coming to her from "Tintagel." Instead, it is Austin Roxburgh who comes to her home as a summer border, talking of Van Diemen's Land. He scorns Tintagel as "nearby." Austin once tried to write a novel, but because his characters rejected him he burned the manuscript and went back to studying the classics. In time Austin asks and receives permission to marry Ellen and, with his mother as co-teacher, proceeds to educate her.

The reader learns these facts in flashbacks. The story proper begins in the middle of things. The Roxburghs have traveled from England to Van Diemen's Land to visit Austin's brother. In a prologue to the main action of the novel the Roxburghs are discussed by the Merivales and Miss Scrimshaw, who have come to see them off on the return journey. The Merivales have migrated from England to New South Wales, where Mrs. Merivale tries to behave in close approximation to an English lady back home in Winchester. Her friend, Miss Scrimshaw, has dared to hint at something untoward between Mr. Roxburgh's brother Garnet and Mrs. Roxburgh. They all agree that Ellen Roxburgh is strange— one of those Cornish "dark people" (15).

Miss Scrimshaw was right in her intuitions about Ellen Roxburgh. Her brother-in-law, a widower, easily seduced her during the visit, and the novelist adds in apparent defense of the woman's indifference that Ellen "could only have admitted to carrying away a cold, consummated lust" (117). Later Garnet signals his awareness of Ellen's potential and their similarities: "You and I would enter hell the glorious way if you could overcome your prudery." Ellen responds coolly: "I hope to redeem myself through my husband—an honourable man, as even you who love him, must admit" (137).

The entry in Ellen's journal about the matter, however, is more honest. She writes: "Only heartening to know that whatever bad I find in myself is of no account beside the positive evil I discover in others. I do not mean the instinctive brutality of the human beast, but the considered evil of a calculating mind. When I say 'others' I mean An Other (and no fiend imagined on the moor at dusk in inexperienced girlhood)" (138). That evening at dinner, which must be shared with her one-time lover, Ellen first wraps herself tightly in her fringed shawl, drawing it over her bosom. Then she changes her mind and drapes it loosely over her shoulders.

During the voyage Ellen admits much to her journal. For example, she confesses to being "intocksicated by a sense of freedom, of pure joy" (69). Of the Captain, who has tried to caution her about the weather of the moment, she writes: "Good, kind, tedjus men make me feel guilty." She also notes that she is "given to fits of drunkenness without having indulged" (70).

In contrast to Ellen's spontaneity—and poor spelling—Mr. Roxburgh writes in his journal of "the blackness in which it is never possible to distinguish the outline of a beloved form, or know the wife of one's own choosing!" He admits he is experiencing "doubt, anguish, even terror . . . to explore which might prove disastrous." He also makes a confession: "I am from time to time the original Abyss, into which I must restrain my rational self from plunging for fear of the consequences" (68). Then overcome by guilt by what he is writing, he obliterates most of it and goes back to reading his beloved Virgil. Obviously there are both overt and latent tensions between the husband and wife.

During the crisis aboard ship, as a bad storm escalates, Ellen tells her husband that she is pregnant. When it is necessary to abandon the brig, she appears on deck wearing her modest jewels, including a garnet ring. Mr. Roxburgh is uncertain of the propriety of adornments at such a time but soon they laugh together, being "temporarily possessed by an almost sensual indifference to their fate" (185).

The following days in the small lifeboat—one of two—to which the Roxburghs have been assigned are fully exploited by the novelist. To be confined in a small space surrounded by an infinite ocean with all the time in the world to consult one's conscience approximates being in Hell. To stay alive becomes the primary good; thus cooperation and individualism vie with each other, depending upon the moment, but benevolence is quite rare.

During an interval on land—unsuitable land so the two boats have to be repaired and launched again—Ellen uses her shawl to sop up rain water she finds in a rock saucer. The second mate, Mr. Pilcher, surprises her in the act. He behaves rudely, tearing through the woman's defenses to find the former servant girl. He asks for and receives disdainfully her garnet ring. The ritual suggests a marriage of conspirators, with Ellen purchasing Pilcher's silence about the selfish use of her shawl. "Now you, too," Ellen quips, "can be counted among the capitalists" (222).

When a youthful member of the crew—no more than a boy—is accidentally drowned while trying to catch shellfish for Ellen, she watches helplessly. Later she tells her husband: "I loved him" (226). Mr. Roxburgh is confused and frightened by his wife's intensity, and the situation deteriorates even more when the survivors set out again. Pilcher cuts the line between the two lifeboats, leaving the Roxburghs' boat to flounder on its own. The distance between their boat and Pilcher's grows greater and greater until Pilcher's pinnace, upon which they had depended, disappears. The novelist insists on the significance, locating it in Ellen's awareness: "Faith in integrity persisted while the rope held, but with the severing of the hawser and gradual disappearance of the faster boat, the horizon had become clouded with doubts" (226).

Mrs. Roxburgh promptly gives birth in the boat to a stillborn child. The Captain, who is gradually losing his mind, reads a service from the drowned boy's Bible as Ellen's child is put to sea in the boy's "glory bag." Not surprisingly, she survives and soon regains her strength: "She would have got to her feet like any other beast of nature, steadying herself in the mud and trampled grass, had it been a field and not a water-logged boat" (230).

After the steward Spurgeon dies, his body is tossed overboard without a service, for the Captain is no longer aware of what is happening. When finally a quiet-appearing shore is sighted, it seems for a short time that all might yet be well. They land, hoping to reach the closest settlement, Moreton Bay, on foot. Soon, however, hostile natives attack the group, killing the Captain and Mr. Roxburgh. The latter's grisly death as the result of a spear through his neck pierces his wife symbolically, killing something in her also. She realizes that she will never pray again.

When the survivors are imprisoned by the natives, Ellen is turned over to the black women and girls and stripped of her clothing and jewelry. Naked and alone when her tormenters run off for a moment, Ellen feels "entirely liberated" (244). Nevertheless, she fashions a fringe of vine leaves to wear around her waist. Into this improvised garment she threads her wedding ring, the only thing left to her from the past.

Confined to a hut by the savage women, Ellen is forced to nurse a sick child. Although the child rejects Ellen's dry breast with a painful bite, Ellen continues to hold the child in her arms. She is aware of missing "absent faces and familiar voices" (247). Soon her "abstract hunger" fades as biological hunger turns into a lust for food. When the savages throw her a leftover piece of fish, she sucks on it desperately and afterwards licks "her deliciously rank fingers," meanwhile whimpering "once or twice to herself" (248).

Ellen's captors eventually hack off her hair with a shell, smear her body with rancid animal fat and charcoal, and plaster her bleeding scalp with wax and feathers. The savage women then admire "their work of art" (251). Although treated at first as a slave, Ellen soon begins to participate in tribal events, and for the duration of her captivity "the spirit of Ellen Gluyas" comes to "Mrs. Roxburgh's rescue" (263). She climbs trees, grows ecstatic over "a fragment of snake-flesh" (266), and begins "to share with these innocent savages an unexpectedly spiritual experience . . . " (271). In the climactic moment of her initiation into savagery she eats human flesh, and is startled that "tasting flesh from the human thigh-bone in the stillness of a forest morning had nourished not only her animal body but some darker need of the hungry spirit" (274).

Ellen is also frankly attracted to the bodies and stench of

the male savages, and when the tribe moves to the mainland she goes along without resisting. There she notices a giant whom she admires. She guesses rightly that he is a convict escaped from a penal colony along the coast. In a private moment they exchange names and other information. She persuades her new friend, whose name is Jack Chance, to take her to Moreton Bay, where she promises she will secure a pardon for him. When Jack doubts that he would be pardoned, the reasonable Ellen Roxburgh argues that "it would be unjust and unnatural." Jack replies: "Men is unnatural and unjust" (281). Nevertheless he eventually agrees.

Ellen's Enlightenment

The long flight through the jungle back to civilization is the heart of the novel and the heart of enlightenment for Ellen. Forced at first to sleep with Jack for safety's sake, she eventually sleeps with him as his lover. During the day Jack hunts for the food which he cooks for her at night. He cares for her and entertains her. He tells her of his life and of the crime that made him a convict. He confesses that he murdered his unfaithful wife.

One day Ellen cries for all the sadness in the world. That night Jack begins "to handle her as though she had been a wheelbarrow, or black woman," in the native manner of sexual intercourse as she has observed in her "adoptive family" (298). When she objects, Jack takes a Laurentian approach: "Two bodies that trust can't do hurt to each other" (298). Ellen, longing for tenderness, is not sure, for the Mrs. Roxburgh part of her knows Ellen is untrustworthy. Soon, however, Ellen allows him to detach her fringe of leaves. When he asks about the ring threaded to one of the vines, she panics and becomes hysterical in her attempt to retrieve the symbol of marriage. Her physical aggression is answered by his physical passion, and the scene ends in the satisfying of their "shared hunger" (299).

Warned by Jack that they must hurry on or run the risk of being recaptured, Ellen hesitates, "hoping to arrive at layers of experience deeper still, which he alone knew how to induce" (300). Ellen is open to the moment. Beside her the old fringe of leaves lies "defoliated," although her ring is still attached to it. Ellen acts. She makes herself a new fringe from fresh vines. This new fringe, the novelist asserts, is "tougher, the leaves furnishing it more leathery than those which had served her thus far" (300–301). Ellen threads her ring onto the vine strands instead of replacing it on her hand, rationalizing that her finger has grown too thin and shrunken to wear the ring safely.

When they set off again Ellen follows Jack, admiring his "lean, disdainful buttocks" (302). She sings a ballad "for her deliverer" (303). Jack imitates bird calls. That night she gives herself to Jack fully, encouraging him "to enter her body" as she presses "her mouth into his." The scene is prolonged, and the novelist comments astringently at the end of the love-night: "After they had fallen apart, they continued soothing each other with the hands of hardened criminals" (307).

In a moment of daring Ellen climbs a tall tree. Jack pursues her, and from their high vantage point they can see a house and a ploughed field. Although their journey's end is near, they hesitate, and that night Jack confesses to Ellen that he slit his wife's throat. As Jack demands Ellen's verdict, he puts his hands around her throat. Does she find him innocent or guilty? Ellen temporizes. Although Jack is satisfied and affirms their mutual understanding, Ellen wonders if he might also suspect her and "kill her in the night with his little axe" (324). Predictably she is more reserved in her lovemaking that evening. "She must keep in mind that tomorrow she would again become Mr. Austin Roxburgh's widow, and must plead, not for a murderer, but a man to whom she owed her life" (325).

The next morning Jack decides not to go as far as the farmhouse with Ellen. At the last moment she loses her fringe of leaves and the wedding ring attached to it, and she is reminded of a picture she once saw in a book in her husband's library: the inhabitants of the Cities of the Plains fleeing naked in one another's arms. After Jack leaves her at the edge of the farm, Ellen is received kindly if with considerable astonishment by strangers, who eventually take her to Moreton Bay.

Although there is no Holstius waiting for Ellen as there was
for Theodore Goodman in *The Aunt's Story*, there is Miss
Scrimshaw, who opportunely has come to visit the family of
the commandant of the post. She soon finds suitable attire for
Ellen, including a bonnet from which the flowers have been
stripped. To Miss Scrimshaw Ellen is a lady in mourning. From
now on she is again "Mrs. Roxburgh."

The authorities are cool but polite as they listen to Mrs.
Roxburgh's incredible narrative. Her plea for Jack is received
with ironic reservations by the commandant. He also insists
on a meeting between Mrs. Roxburgh and Mr. Pilcher, the
sole survivors of the wreck. Survivors, perforce, are always
special. As the only reliable witnesses to a catastrophe they
become accidentally significant. Also, survivors have presumably been saved by God. As the elected, they feel both
pride and guilt, knowing that God is always thanked by the
living while the dead, who might have cursed Him, are mute.

When Pilcher notes that they must have been "favoured
by Providence" (377), Ellen suggests that since neither one
of them may ever speak the real truth about the event, they
might as well be friends. Pilcher does not understand.
Although he remains protected by his clichés and is building
a chapel as a thank-you to God, he is now willing to admit
that he hated Roxburgh and his wife. When he returns Mrs.
Roxburgh's garnet ring, she tosses it out of the window.

Ellen Roxburgh's final ordeal begins with a visit from the
chaplain. Confronted by his complacency, she shudders, admitting that she is quite uncertain about her Christian commitments. The chaplain tries to engage her in prayer but she
suddenly screams as she hallucinates Jack being punished,
whereupon the man of God flees the scene. Later Mrs. Roxburgh goes to visit the chapel that Pilcher is building by
hand. The irony is heavy as she notes that "God is Love" is
printed over the altar.

Mrs. Roxburgh's passage home is assured with the help of
Miss Scrimshaw, at least as far as Sydney. Miss Scrimshaw,
who has emerged as strong, confides in her friend that she
has always wanted to be an eagle: "To reach the heights!"
Mrs. Roxburgh, however, the novelist explains, "remains in-
eluctably earthbound" (402).

And so it comes to pass that the widow Roxburgh may marry a Mr. Jevons who accompanies them on the trip to Sydney, an up-and-coming city where the middle-aged Mr. and Mrs. Jevons would be comfortable while, the novelist archly affirms, Miss Scrimshaw continues to look for "any circumstantial straw which may indicate an ordered universe" (405). Mr. Roxburgh, had he not been dead and thus muted, would probably have quoted Virgil at this fragile moment: "Happy is he who has unveiled the cause of things, and who can ignore inexorable Fate and the roar of insatiate Hell" (34).

Stripped of Sectarian Sacking

White used a real incident as a springboard for his novel. A Mrs. Eliza Fraser had actually survived a shipwreck in May, 1836, near the Great Barrier Reef. Her eventual rescue, the stories she told, and the stories that were told about her became something of a legend.[4] White, however, deviates considerably from both the recorded facts and the subsequent legends. Thus *A Fringe of Leaves* troubled those who found White's plot ridiculous, contrasting it with the more credible fictions of Scott or Melville. Others were frankly surprised that he had chosen to compete with these earlier greats.

As a matter of simple fact, White was not competing with the past or the present. Most of all he has never liked historical novels. In 1980, in an address at the National Book Council awards, he explained how and why he has altered the conventions of the genre. Although he was willing to take "a historic character or moment" as his "starting point" in *Voss* and *A Fringe of Leaves*, he never did intend to re-create history. Rather, his objective has been to "preserve psychological credibility" while respecting his "aesthetic principles." His conclusion reflects his confidence in his own work: "If instead of writing *Voss*, I had written a novel about Leichhardt, in whose life there was no woman his obsessive equal, or if in *A Fringe of Leaves* I hadn't substituted Ellen Roxburgh for Eliza Fraser, little more than a hardbitten shrew from the Orkneys, neither novel would have had the psychological complexities, the sensibility, and the passion I was able to explore."⁵

Such explorations take on the appearance of religious fervor, but White's intensities are far from the cool dogmas of any orthodoxy. William Walsh, who likes *A Fringe of Leaves*, finds it comparable to the novels of D. H. Lawrence. In a comfortable phrase he finds it "stripped of sectarian sacking."⁶ Neither Lawrence nor White, however, are credible witnesses to anything other than what Albert Camus has called the "benign indifference of the universe." Furthermore, White's lovers do not quite ignite Lawrence's "pentecost flame" in their sexual intercourse. Ellen's frank sensuality is not the refined abandon of a suppressed Lady Chatterley. Besides, more than once she feels like a "hardened criminal." Also, White's Ellen does not romanticize the savages. She enjoys their savagery as honest but has no illusions about their primeval nobility. Neither does White, apparently, and his novel has been compared unfavorably with the works of other Australian writers, some of whom penetrate the heart of darkness and find beautiful primitives, while others take a dry, sociological approach to the aborigines and their ways.

Katharine Prichard, for example, published a novel in 1929 based on her own experiences in the Australian outback. Prichard's *Coonardoo* keeps close to facts as it explores a native woman's problems with white men—and with her own sensuality.⁷ Another novelist, Eleanor Dark, tried to demonstrate that the "abos" are spiritually superior to the white Australians, and her fiction is pleasing to those sentimentalists who need to rationalize their own guilt.⁸

In contrast, Patrick White's concerns are less partisan and more humanistic. White's Jack Chance is, of course, not an Australian native. He is an English convict whose blackness connotes little more than a color-cover so that he can mingle with the real natives undetected. Whereas Dark and Prichard empathize with natives, White concentrates on Jack's status as a convict and his relationship with society and Ellen.

Much depends upon the reader's set toward White's habit of deflating an ecstatic moment by an abrupt return to humdrum things. Ellen's liberation, which would be impossible for any decent white woman in the past century, is not as farfetched today. White chose to combine the jungle of a past time with modern sensibilities. He also knew how to offend those sensibilities. For example, Ellen does not reject human flesh any more than a Christian rejects a communion wafer—which allegedly has been magically transformed into God's flesh!

Anyway, White deflates Ellen's epiphanies when he returns her to civilization. He gives her one peaceful moment in the God-is-Love chapel but she is too intelligent to abide with such clichés for long, and in the end Ellen is quite willing to resume many of the hypocrisies of her pre-jungle life. Her ordeals enlightened her but did not redeem her. It is the reader who may cling to the agonies and ecstasies after the novelist has finished with Ellen, for Ellen was only a means to an experience—the reader's experience. Patrick White has not pretended here to be anything other than an artist. There is no real Ellen. All is illusion, word patterns, and verbal flourishes, which in the end succeed or fail on their own terms.

Messages in Thunder:
Big Toys and *The Night the Prowler*

White's drama, *The Season at Sarsaparilla*, was revived in 1976 at the Sydney Opera House. The event was successful enough to encourage the playwright in White, and in 1977 he had another drama ready for production. *Big Toys* was directed by Jim Sharman, who had also directed the revival of *The Season*. The three characters in the new drama were played by members of the former production, so that, all in all, White's new play was a kind of family affair designed to please those whom White had previously pleased. It was, in fact, a critical success but, predictably, not a popular one.

The text of *Big Toys* has been published in Sydney, with a perceptive introduction by Katharine Brisbane, who admires White but also admits that all of his plays have been controversial, especially the four produced in the 1960s, which were judged to be "alien to current convention."[9] By 1976,

however, the Australian theater had been belatedly liberated
and White's dramatic unconventionalities were no longer as
alien. His choice of a subject in *Big Toys* was frankly didac-
tic, even preachy, and thus limited in popular appeal. In
1964 White left his goat woman on Bald Mountain experiencing a vision of the future which tempered despair with
hope. There was then a chance that humanity would not
destroy itself. In *Big Toys* he exchanges the mountain for a
penthouse in a fashionable suburb of Sydney, and the play
itself is mostly a platform from which the dramatist lectures
his audience on political and economic evils.

The big toys of the title are the rewards and bribes that
sophisticated people use to get what they want or to keep
what they have. The assumption is that everyone can be purchased or at least persuaded to be a "mellow witness" (46).
The toys range from jewels, cars, sex, and flattery to the
uranium which is needed in big bombs. Even sincerity has
become a device to defeat someone else, and honesty has
been debased to a technique for controlling others.

In contrast to contemporary uses and abuses of friendship,
the old Australian mateship would seem preferable. Thus
White finds himself in something of a dilemma, for he had
long ago expressed his distrust of mateship. Now it seems
that something was lost when mates became suspicious of
their love for one another as either homoerotic or exploita-
tive. Lost innocence is still lost, nevertheless, and there is no
turning back.

The two men in *Big Toys* do in fact embrace at one point,
and their relationship ends with one male kissing the other
on the mouth—sardonically as well as erotically. Terry
Legge, a working-class Marxist, and Richard Bosanquet, a
wealthy Queen's Counsel, are not overtly homosexual,
however, and Richard's wife, although dishonest and seduc-
tive, is not really a whore. Yet in the tangle of emotions that
is the plot of this play, each one of the three characters learns
to suspect his own motives and psychological health. In the
end, when the Marxist refuses to accept an expensive auto-
mobile as a reward for mellowing his testimony against a
former mate who has cornered the uranium market, the
point is neither clear nor shining bright. Terry has already

slept with Richard's wife, and she, poor soul, finally accepts the rejected car as another one of her expensive toys. When Terry leaves her, she looks out from the terrace of her penthouse, then turns her back on the night, and "soundlessly" cries: "Christ . . . Oh Christ . . . " as "the stage darkens" (58). Brisbane calls *Big Toys* black comedy, defending it as "the perfect form in which to express such a message of thunder."[xii]

Meanwhile, White himself wrote the script for a screenplay version of his short story, "The Night the Prowler," which was filmed in the same year *Big Toys* appeared.[10] Also directed by Sharman, it was only a qualified success. The short story was lengthened, scenes opened out, and the message made more explicit, but the thunder in both *Big Toys* and *The Night the Prowler*, impressive as it seems in its rumblings, is not as potent as the lightning that blazes from White's next novel, *The Twyborn Affair*, published in 1979.

The Twyborn Affair: Eudoxia

Joan and Curly Golson, rich middle-aged Australians on holiday in Europe, have chosen on the recommendation of Lady Tewkes the Grand Hotel Splendide des Ligures as their residence during their visit to the French Riviera. The Golsons, both of whom are in trade—"Golson's Emporium" and "Sewell's Sweat-free Hats" respectively, in Sydney—are insecure provincials when in England. On the Continent things are somewhat better: "To land at Calais or Boulogne and find oneself simply and unacceptably foreign was by contrast a relief."[11] Joan Golson's curiosity about a Madame Eudoxia Vatatzes, who is living in a villa near the Hotel Splendide with an elderly, pre-senile Greek exile, is keen but also ingenuous, for she does not know that Eudoxia is the son of her friend, Eadie, with whom she once shared a homoerotic episode.

The novelist takes his time zooming in on his hero, first introducing "her" via Joan's window-peeking at the villa one day when Joan's rented car is delayed by a blown-out tire along the road where the Vatatzes live. Joan uses the occasion to observe from just beyond the roadside hedge the fascinating couple inside the villa. An old man and what appears to be a tall, handsome young woman are seated at the piano side by side, playing a duet. Joan is a romantic: " . . . the lithe young woman and the stiff, elderly man—the lovers; there was by now no doubt in Mrs. Golson's mind" (17).

The same scene is replayed later, with a difference, in Eudoxia's journal, dated "7 Feb. 1914." Eudoxia and her "husband" have seen the peeker, disagree on Mrs. Golson's motivation but know that she is "Eadie's pal." They both deplore the invasion, and in her journal Eudoxia describes the incident as disastrous: "Everything, I now see, has been leading up to this act of aggression. Gentle perfection is never allowed to last for long. The more laboriously it has been built up, the more painfully it is brought down" (22).

Obviously Eudoxia is given to hyperbolic reactions. The reader is not informed at this time, however, about the background coincidences and therefore does not know much more than Joan Golson does about Eudoxia and what she is referring to when she writes in her journal:

Why am I besotted on this elderly, dotty, in many ways tiresome Greek? I can only think it's because we have been made for each other, that our minds as well as our bodies fit, every bump to every cranny, and quirk to quirk. If I hate him at times it's because I hate myself. If I love him more deeply than I love E. it's because I know this other creature too well, and cannot rely entirely on him or her. (23)

It seems that Angelos, the old Greek, really loves Eudoxia. He has given her a "pomegranate shawl" and a "spangled fan," with which she likes to amuse herself. She confesses to her journal that she likes to see herself in the glass, playing with these feminine artifacts: "Looked at myself in the glass and decided I would pass. As I do! Or, at any rate, on the days when I don't hate—when I can forgive myself for being me" (23).

Joan finally meets Eudoxia by accident, quite literally, when Eudoxia twists her ankle outside the Golson's hotel and is rescued by Joan. As a reward, the Golsons are invited to a tea party at the villa, which turns into a rout because of the old man's petulance. Meanwhile, other journal entries describe Eudoxia's childhood and its traumas, including her love for her father and her subsequent attachment to the old Greek, partly as father-surrogate.

The first part of the novel ends when Eudoxia's Greek suddenly dies after the couple have left the villa and taken lodgings in a pensione. Angelos's last words, overheard by the landlady, expose Eudoxia: "I have had from you, dear boy, the only happiness I've ever known" (126). Eudoxia therefore leaves immediately and is not heard from again until she appears in "Part Two" as Lieutenant Eddie Twyborn.

Eddie

"Eddie" is somewhat of a hero on his way home to Australia at the end of World War I, and he becomes the center of much interest on board the ship. He is an attractive man, still young enough to excite unattached females. Although willing to be penetrated sexually by him, the women have no chance to reciprocate, for he remains impenetrable both symbolically and literally.

At home Eddie renews and quickens into new problems his relationship with his mother and his father. The visit sets the occasion for flashbacks which more or less account for Eudoxia-Eddie's unusual behavior. For example, Eddie's father, Judge Edward Twyborn, was affectionate toward his boy-child only once, during a moment in which the lad was lying in bed, warm and wet with his own spilled urine. Not much could come of such limited parental support.

The returned officer decides to leave home again and try roughing it as a jackeroo on a ranch, ostensibly to reinforce his new maleness. Eddie's father uses influence with a friend, Greg Lushington, and in the sequel Eddie is accepted as an apprentice hand and as an assistant to the manager on Lushington's sheep ranch. There his quarters are austere and his assignments astringent.

As chance would have it—chance again being White's providence—Eddie's boss is Don Prowse, a not unattractive red-haired fellow recently deserted by his wife and in his own way as lonely and as tentative as Eddie. The relationship between Prowse and Eddie gradually accelerates into a sexual affair which climaxes just twice, the first time in a contact which is most efficiently described as the rape-with-consent of Eddie by Prowse, the second time as the reciprocal rape-with-consent of Prowse by Eddie. The retribution reverses the crime, and the affair ends.

Meanwhile, Eddie has been having a male-female affair with the boss's wife, Marcia Lushington, a complicated involvement which emotionally affects both Marcia's husband and Don Prowse, who once fathered one of Marcia's children, now deceased. At this time Eddie's training as a jackeroo is interrupted by a long period of recovery from a fall from a horse, during which he becomes dependent upon the peasant woman who cooks for him. He also moves closer to his boss, Greg Lushington, and comes to love him in one of his several ways of loving. After events reach an impasse, Eddie leaves the ranch, turning up later as the owner and manager of a fashionable brothel in London. He has now become Eadith, a procuress. Eadith remembers, however, having been both Eudoxia and Eddie. Thus the new heroine is an accumulated personality. Appropriately, the texture of the writing becomes increasingly rich and lyrical as the reader is invited to make connections.

Eadith

Settled in Chelsea in a good section of London for her business, Eadith Trist has learned to prefer "the hour when dawn takes over from darkness" (309). She likes to walk through the streets, coming "to terms with reality between the two dawns in the deserted park. Somewhere between the fragrant scent of fresh cowpats and the reek of human excrement" (310). After her walks she returns to Beckwith Street, to "the house she owned thanks to her patron, into the atmosphere of spent cigarettes, stale cigar, dried semen (and again, human shit)" (310).

The seasoned Eadith has absorbed the more ingenuous Eddie, who as a hard-muscled fellow in dungarees had tried to stabilize his role as a male. Eadith's goal is to become an efficient whore-mistress whose girls give good value to her distinguished and demanding guests. Upon her return to London she has easily exchanged Eddie's accessories and jeans for cosmetics and dresses. Sexual activity for its own sake, however, has been deleted from her life. She is described as "too disgusted with herself, and human beings in general, ever to want to dabble in sex again, let alone aspire to that great ambivalence, love. She could only contemplate it as an abstraction, an algebra" (311).

The details of how Eddie became Mrs. Trist are not all supplied but the main facts are eventually filled in. Capable of compassion, if not love, she is grateful for the friendship of her patron, Lord Gravenor. Nevertheless, she no longer takes off her inner layer of clothing before anyone, including her assistant, Ada. Eadith still possesses male genitals, of course, which on occasion still behave autonomously in male ways—the aftermath of sticky thighs and all—yet she refuses Lord Gravenor's physical advances to the end of their relationship even though he may have by then suspected, even needed, her male anatomy.

Just before the end of the novel, a finely etched moment occurs in the park one day. Resting on a park bench, Eadith's mother, 'Eadie', notices a familiar-looking lady seated near her. She hands the lady (who is Eadith) a note asking: "Are you my son Eddie?" The answer, penciled hurriedly by Eadith, is what it must be: "No, but I am your daughter Eadith" (422).

After a short pause the mother adds one more line to the dialogue and quietly replies: "I am so glad. I've always wanted a daughter" (423).

The Hero as Himself

Near the very end of his jest and joust with cosmic indifference the novelist allows the Twyborn hero to return once again to his male role—at least to a male costume. He happens to be walking through London at the moment that World War II quickens into killing. He has forgotten to remove the heavy makeup that he has been using for years as the madam of a fashionable London brothel. He has, however, reverted to men's clothes and a short haircut. He is, in a word, a grotesque.

White's word choices in the terminal moments of this novel—the hero's mother, another Twyborn complexity, gets the very last scenes and lines—are carefully equivocal.

The rites are both a defeat and a celebration for the hero Eudoxia-become-Eddie-become-Eadith-become-Eddie. The last Eddie Twyborn is on his way to see his mother, whom he has recently found again after a long separation.

It is important to accept the fact that Eddie's mother is named "Eadie," and thus is easily confused by name with her offspring. When Eddie changes to Eadith, he is closer to being his mother, and by the same token the mother is also closer to being the son when he is her daughter. (As an additional distraction, White named the hero's father Edward!)

The first moment of the Twyborn hero's final passage across London is vintage-White:

As he crossed this seemingly deserted city, a scapegoat again in search of sacrifice, his steely tonsure parried the steely evening light. He glanced sideways through the gathering dusk and saw himself reflected in plate-glass: the distorted shoulders of the shoddy suit, the pointed shoes, the cropped hair. He was disgusted to see he had forgotten to take off Eadith's make-up. The great magenta mouth was still flowering in a chalk face shaded with violet, the eyes overflowing mascara banks, those of a distressed woman, professional whore, or hopeful amateur lover. (428)

Eddie notices a "fiery razzle-dazzle" in the east (428). This "perverse sunset" is a fire set off by a bomb. He also hears "the chuffing of his own heart, a clangour of racing engines, the thump and crump of history becoming unstable, crumbling" (428).

Relieved that at last the war is substantial enough to see and feel, Eddie rejoices in the fact that "they" will now learn that London was never really theirs anyway. As his "share in time" is about to be "snatched away" via a fragment of a bomb, he remembers episodes from his past. Allusions to places and events mentioned earlier in the novel now redefine time, changing it from a line with direction to a kind of mandala. The novelist transmutes the hero's memories into a total awareness of the present, "all contained in this great unstable temporal house, all but Eddie and Eadith, unless echoes of their voices threading pandemonium" (429).

This time the Twyborn hero is about to run the wrong way

into death. In World War I he ran an equally wrong way into the battle and ironically received a medal for bravery: "So he prepared to advance alone into this brick no-man's-land. This time could it be despair running in the wrong direction?" Yes and no, the novelist implies, for he is no longer "able to move from his position on the pavement" (429).

When Eddie at first thinks the detached hand he sees after he is thrown to the ground by the explosion is that of a soldier who was passing by, he checks on reality and finds the soldier's hands are still attached to "bristling wrists" (429). And then he looks again: "It was his own hand he saw as he ebbed, incredibly, away from it" (430).

What could a hero say then? The true hero must relinquish all claims to heroism to be a true hero. That is, no hero behaves heroically. In this case the hero says something both relevant and flippant. He remembers that Ada, his assistant at the whorehouse, has been stockpiling against the threat of wartime scarcity. Among the things hoarded is a carton of band-aids. And so the hero's last words are: "Fetch me a bandaid, Ada." His ultimate fate is then vaguely specified as "flowing onward, on to wherever the crimson current might carry him" (430).

Meanwhile, Eadie, weary of waiting for her new daughter, walks out into the garden of her hotel (as Eddie lies dead in the street). There she observes a little bird, "A bulbul . . . perched on the rim of the stone bird-bath, dipping his beak." Then he shakes "his little jester's cap" and raises "his beak towards the sun" (432).

A Band-aid

The novelist's anguish and irony have peaked in the Twyborn hero. It is not easy, however, to adjust to the switching pronouns, and there is no relief until near the end of the long novel, when the hero becomes "he" and "him" for the last time. It should be noted emphatically, however, that the hero never alters his physiological identifications of maleness. His orgasms, some of which are detailed as onanism, are always "normal" in location and sensation. His transvestism is exactly that, the mere changing of outer clothing. As a woman, the hero is shy about his feet, which are naturally too big for a woman's shoes. He must also use depilatories and heavy makeup to conceal his body hair. It is thus not a fact, within the novel, that the hero is ever a woman, for his-her basic maleness does not vary much no matter which costume—or band-aid—the hero is wearing.

Ideally, the Twyborn hero would not behave perversely, and it follows logically, therefore, that often he does not behave sexually at all as the least perverse way to respond to his lust. Because love is always more or less perverse, however, insofar as it parodies or debases or frustrates or exaggerates sexuality, the Twyborn hero is forced into certain perversities when in love.

Of the three epigraphs chosen by the novelist for *The Twyborn Affair* one is attributed to Diane Arbus: "Sometimes you'll see someone with nothing on but a bandaid." The other two, attributed to David Malouf and Jorge Luis Borges, both refer to anxiety about the future, the former to "the mystery of what we have not yet become," the latter to the possibility that Heaven has been "overrated by theologians" and that "even in Hell the damned are not always satisfied."

The Twyborn Affair is not an easy novel to classify, let alone judge. Nevertheless, Walsh has conscientiously tried: "Not the best nor the worst, not a *Voss* nor a *Riders in the Chariot,* perhaps something between *The Vivisector* and *The Eye of the Storm, The Twyborn Affair* still has about it a creative glow and a capacity to deal with the depths and the distances of the human psyche." White shows "the solitariness of the human person . . . and the simultaneous melting of categories, the dissolution of boundaries and edges which the living of life entails."[12]

An American critic recognizes that the novel is "a case study of sexual proteanism, and the thematic core is the mystery of human identity." Yet he concludes that it is not "a wholly satisfying novel. The problem is the book's unremitting scorn of human attachment."[13] Another American critic cries out against the novel, calling it "an imposing dud." To make assurance doubly sure, he adds: "*The Twyborn Affair* is the worst novel by a writer of any repute that I have recently read."[14]

Nicholas Mosley, after sympathetically reviewing *The Twyborn Affair*, praises White's "consciousness, elegance, and wisdom," and his "wonderfully witty and allusive style . . . which can describe both disgusting things and transcendental things with empathy and detachment." Mosley's final judgment: "He has one foot on the earth and the other heaven knows where—which is a good position for any colossus."[15] But it's the "heaven knows where" that remains too elusive for many readers. To what extent is *The Twyborn Affair* a defiant gesture? How seriously must it be taken before it is decoded? And what price band-aid?

In his 1981 "self-portrait," *Flaws in the Glass*, White says that in his opinion his "three best novels are *The Solid Mandala, The Aunt's Story*, and *The Twyborn Affair*." He defends the three works unequivocally: "All three say something more than what is sacred to Aust. Lit. [*sic*] For this reason some of them were ignored in the beginning, some reviled and dismissed as pornography. After years two of them were accepted; it remains to be seen what will become of *The Twyborn Affair*."[16]

Patrick White as Prophet

In 1980, in an essay which was expanded into his book-length self-portrait, White tried to explain himself:

What do I believe? I'm accused of not making it explicit. How to be explicit about an overreaching grandeur, a daily wrestling match with an opponent whose limbs never become material, whose blood and sweat are scattered on the pages of anything the serious writer writes. Whose essence is contained less in what is said than in the silences. In patterns on water. A gust of wind. A flower opening. I hesitate to add a child, because a child can grow into a monster, a destroyer. Am I a destroyer?, [*sic*] this face in the glass which has spent a lifetime searching for what it believes, but can never prove the truth. A face consumed by wondering whether truth can be the worst destroyer of all.[17]

For those still anxious to prove that White is some kind of Christian, or at least—perhaps at best—a religious person despite his unorthodoxies, the writer's own conjecture that he may be a "destroyer" is disturbing. That White has enjoyed being controversial is quite apparent in his autobiography. His honest identification of himself as essentially homosexual is not, however, an invitation to overemphasize the possible effect of his sexual preferences on his writing.

Sublimation or rationalizing his deviation—as some would say—White identifies the only relevant component of his difference from the majority of men: "I see myself not so much a homosexual as a mind possessed by the spirit of man or woman according to actual situations or the characters I become in my writing."[18] This statement points to hermaphroditism or androgyny as the proper condition of the creative spirit. Because White has endorsed himself as an artist capable of creating out of himself works that transcend his own disabilities—he calls them "flaws"—he has needed to explain how his dedication to passion and compassion has not led him into disaster. "What drives me," he concludes, "is sensual, emotional, instinctive. At the same time I like to think creative reason reins me in as I reach the edge of disaster" (81).

White has asserted often that he has rejected organized religion. He has, however, admitted that the ideas and images of Jung, for example, stimulate religious impulses in him. Also, although he has called Westminster Abbey a "grisly museum" and St. Peter's in Rome a "great rococo bed for an operatic courtesan," he has had "inklings" of "what one always hopes for" in Ayia Sophia in Constantinople, in the Parthenon—"alone on a winter afternoon"—in a Friends' Meeting House, in "a garden full of birds, in my own silent room." His conclusion defines the importance of his writings not only to himself but also to many less articulate admirers, and is also a fit conclusion for this study: "The ultimate spiritual union is probably as impossible to achieve as the perfect work of art or the unflawed human relationship. In matters of faith, art, and love I have had to reconcile myself to starting again where I began" (74).

Notes and References

Chapter One

1. *Flaws in the Glass: A Self-Portrait* (New York, 1981); hereafter page references cited in the text in parentheses.
2. White's mother once called him a freak because he refused to go to a cricket match. Others referred to him as a changeling when he was a child. See *Flaws*, p. 43 and p. 5.
3. "The Prodigal Son," *Australian Letters* 1, no. 3 (1958):39.
4. For a recent short story by White see "Fête Galante," *Meanjin Quarterly* 36, no. 1 (1977):3–24.

Chapter Two

1. See Alan Lawson, "Unmerciful Dingoes? The Critical Reception of Patrick White," *Meanjin Quarterly* 32, no. 4 (1973): 379–92.
2. *Flaws in the Glass*, p. 40.
3. See Leon Cantrell, "Patrick White's First Book," *Australian Literary Studies* 6, no. 4 (1974):434–36. Cantrell describes the volume as a "stapled quarto . . . [containing] 48 pages with all edges deckled" (434).
4. *The Ploughman and Other Poems* (Sydney, 1935).
5. *Literary Digest*, Aug. 11, 1934, p. 31, where it is reprinted as "a new face" from *The London Mercury*.
6. White's first novel, *Happy Valley*, begins with the flight of a hawk; his most recent novel, *The Twyborn Affair*, ends with a bulbul "shaking his jester's cap." White also uses eagles, peacocks, and cockatoos as images of strength, vanity, and beauty.
7. See J. R. Dyce, *Patrick White as Playwright* (St. Lucia, Queensland, 1974). I am much indebted to this excellent study for information on White's early experiments in the theater as well as the fates of later productions in Australia.
8. See L. T. Hergenan, "Patrick White's *Return to Abyssinia*," *Australian Literary Studies* 7, no. 4 (1976):421–24. The play opened in London in March 1947, and ran for nearly three weeks.

9. "The Twitching Colonel," *London Mercury* 35, 210 (1937): 602–609; hereafter page references cited in the text in parentheses.
10. "Cocotte," *Horizon* 1 (May 1940):364.
11. *Happy Valley* (New York: Viking, 1940); hereafter page references cited in the text in parentheses.
12. William Walsh, *Patrick White's Fiction* (London, 1977), p. 3.
13. J. S. Southron, *New York Times Book Review*, May 26, 1940, p. 7.
14. *Times Literary Supplement* (London), Feb. 11, 1939, p. 91.
15. Geoffrey Dutton, *Patrick White* (Melbourne, 1963), p. 11.
16. R. F. Brissenden, *Patrick White* (London, 1966), p. 15.
17. *The Living and the Dead* (New York, 1941); hereafter page references cited in the text in parentheses.
18. *Flaws in the Glass*, p. 77.
19. Lawson, "Unmerciful Dingoes?" p. 380.
20. J. S. Southron, *New York Times Book Review*, Feb. 9, 1941, p. 6.
21. *Times Literary Supplement* (London), July 5, 1941, p. 321.
22. Walsh, *Patrick White's Fiction*, p. 16.

Chapter Three

1. *Flaws in the Glass*, p. 127.
2. *Four Plays* (New York, 1966), p. 15; hereafter page references cited in the text in parentheses.
3. Dyce, *Patrick White as Playwright*.
4. H. G. Kippax, *Four Plays by Patrick White* (Melbourne, 1967), p. 3. I am indebted to Kippax for this information. He was the first to reprint White's own program note for the production.
5. Ibid., pp. 3–4.
6. Dyce, *Patrick White as Playwright*, p. 6.
7. See Thelma Herring, "Maenads and Goat-Song: 'The Plays of Patrick White,'" in G. A. Wilkes, ed., *Ten Essays on Patrick White* (Sydney, 1970), pp. 147–62. Herring, in 1965, believed that White might become a great dramatist. The quotation occurs on p. 156.
8. Brian Kiernan, *Patrick White* (New York, 1980), pp. 33–34. Kiernan's perceptive and informed survey of White's work does not benefit from either White's recent autobiography or his novel, *The Twyborn Affair*.
9. *Flaws in the Glass*, p. 25.
10. Ibid., p. 128.

11. *The Aunt's Story* (New York: Viking Compass Books, 1962), p. 3; hereafter page references cited in the text in parentheses.
12. See Patricia A. Morley, *The Mystery of Unity: Theme and Technique in the Novels of Patrick White* (Montreal and London, 1972). Morley finds not only a mystic unity in *The Aunt's Study* but also a mythic framework derived from Homer's *Odyssey*.
13. See Lawson, "Unmerciful Dingoes?" p. 381.
14. Walter Havighurst, *Saturday Review of Literature*, Jan. 3, 1948, p. 11.
15. Peter Beatson, *The Eye in the Mandala* (London, 1976), p. 99.
16. Kiernan, *Patrick White*, p. 32.

Chapter Four

1. "The Prodigal Son," *Australian Letters*, p. 39.
2. Ibid.
3. See *Flaws in the Glass*, p. 40. White did, however, feel "a sense of well-being" in Weimar despite his "lack of sympathy with Weimar's two great poets."
4. *The Tree of Man* (New York, 1955); page references cited in the text in parentheses.
5. Walsh, *Patrick White's Fiction*, p. 40 and p. 38.
6. The poem is from A. E. Housman's "A Shropshire Lad," and begins "On Wenlock's Edge the wood's in trouble . . . /."
7. John McClaren, "The Image of Reality in Our Writing," in *Twentieth Century Australian Literary Criticism*, ed. Clement Semmler (Melbourne, 1967), pp. 239–40.
8. Kiernan, *Patrick White*, p. 49.
9. *Voss* (New York, 1957), p. 3; hereafter page references cited in the text in parentheses. See also *Voss: With Introduction and Notes by H. P. Heseltine* (London: Longmans, Green, 1965), p. 391. This edition contains glossaries of Australian terms, place names, German words and phrases, a map of Ludwig Leichhardt's journeys, a critical essay, an assortment of "issues and problems," and a select bibliography.
10. William Walsh, *Patrick White: Voss. Studies in English Literature, No. 62* (London; Edward Arnold, 1976), pp. 48–49. The assumption in this series was that the reader had already read the work discussed.
11. See Sylvia Gzell, "Themes and Imagery in *Voss* and *Riders in the Chariot*," in *Twentieth Century Australian Literary Criticism*, pp. 252–67.

12. Phoebe Adams, *Atlantic Monthly*, Oct. 1957, p. 184.
13. John Coates, "*Voss* and Jacob Boehme: A Note on the Spirituality of Patrick White," *Australian Literary Studies* 9, no. 1(1979):122. See also Jean-Pierre Durix, "Natural Elements in Patrick White's *Voss*," *World Literature Written in English* 18, no. 2 (1979):345–52.
14. Vivian Smith, *Vance and Nettie Palmer* (Boston: Twayne Publishers, 1975), p. 20.

Chapter Five

1. Ray Willbanks, *Randolph Stow* (Boston: Twayne Publishers, 1978), p. 17.
2. T. Inglis Moore, *Social Patterns in Australian Literature* (Berkeley, 1971), pp. 19–21.
3. Randolph Stow, *To the Islands* (Boston: Little, Brown, 1958), p. 156.
4. *Flaws in the Glass*, p. 104.
5. *Riders in the Chariot* (New York, 1961), n. p.; hereafter page references are cited in the text in parentheses.
6. Kiernan, *Patrick White*, p. 83.
7. See J. F. Burrows, "Archetypes and Stereotypes: *Riders in the Chariot*," in G. A. Wilkes, *Ten Essays on Patrick White*, pp. 47–71. The two quotations are from p. 50 and p. 71.
8. Walsh, *Patrick White's Fiction*, p. 66.
9. Marcel Aurousseau, "Odi Profanum Vulgus: Patrick White's *Riders in the Chariot*," *Meanjin Quarterly* 21, no. 28 (1962):29.
10. *Time*, Oct. 6, 1961, p. 100.
11. *The Solid Mandala* (New York, 1966); page references cited in the text in parentheses.
12. Bernard McCabe, "Messages in Marbles," *Saturday Review*, Feb. 12, 1966, p. 36.
13. A. A. Phillips, "'The Solid Mandala': Patrick White's New Novel," *Meanjin Quarterly* 25, no. 1 (1966):31.
14. Walsh, *Patrick White's Fiction*, pp. 60–61.
15. Walter Havighurst, "A Twice-Told Tale of 2 Brothers," *Chicago Tribune*, Feb. 13, 1966, p. 15.
16. Morley, *The Mystery of Unity*, p. 206.
17. *Flaws in the Glass*, pp. 146–47.

Chapter Six

1. Beatson, *Eye in the Mandala*, p. 167.
2. Ibid., pp. 39–40.

3. Morley, *The Mystery of Unity*, p. 210.
4. *The Vivisector* (New York, 1970), p. 174; hereafter page references are cited in the text in parentheses.
5. Richard N. Coe, "The Artist and the Grocer: Patrick White's 'The Vivisector,'" *Meanjin Quarterly* 29, no. 4 (1970):527.
6. Pryce-Jones, "The Vivisector," *New York Times Book Review*, Nov. 8, 1970, p. 50.
7. Morley, *The Mystery of Unity*, p. 232.
8. Walsh, *Patrick White's Fiction*, p. 110.
9. *The Eye of the Storm* (New York, 1974), p. 71; hereafter page references are cited in the text in parentheses.
10. Beatson, *Eye in the Mandala*, p. 38 and pp. 30–31.
11. George Steiner, "Carnal Knowledge," *New Yorker*, March 4, 1974, pp. 109–13.
12. *Times Literary Supplement* (London), Sept. 21, 1973, p. 1072.
13. See Manly Johnson, "Patrick White: The Eye of the Language," *World Literature Written in English* 15, no 2(1976):339–58.

Chapter Seven

1. See Vincent Buckley, "Towards an Australian Literature," in *Twentieth Century Australian Literary Criticism*, pp. 75–85. Buckley, in 1958, was daring enough to advocate the teaching of "Australian Literature" at the university level.
2. A. A. Phillips, *Henry Lawson* (New York: Twayne Publishers, 1970), p. 138.
3. G. A. Wilkes and J. C. Reid, *The Literatures of the British Commonwealth: Australia and New Zealand*, ed. A. L. McLeod (University Park, 1970), p. 120.
4. All references here are to *The Burnt Ones* (New York, 1964); page references cited in the text in parentheses.
5. All references here are to *The Cockatoos* (New York, 1975); page references cited in the text in parentheses.
6. Rose Marie Beston, "More Burnt Ones: Patrick White's *The Cockatoos*," *World Literature Written in English* 14, no. 2 (1975):520.
7. Eudora Welty, "Patrick White's *The Cockatoos*," in *The Eye of the Story* (New York: Random, 1978), p. 264.
8. Brian Kiernan, "Short Story Chronicle," *Meanjin Quarterly* 34, no. 1 (1975):37.
9. David Myers, *The Peacocks and the Bourgeoise* (Adelaide, 1978), pp. 1, 173.
10. All page references in the text here are to *Four Plays*.

11. Wilkes and Reid, *The Literatures of the British Commonwealth*, p. 129.
12. Ibid., p. 127.
13. Dyce, *Patrick White as Playwright*, pp. 1–2.
14. Walsh, *Patrick White's Fiction*, p. 79.
15. Roderick Cook, *Harper's*, Sept., 1966, p. 114.

Chapter Eight

1. See Thelma Herring and G. A. Wilkes, "A Conversation with Patrick White," *Southerly* 33, no. 2 (1973):132–43. The quotation is from p. 139.
2. Ibid., p. 140.
3. All references in parentheses here are to *A Fringe of Leaves* (New York, 1976). The pagination of this edition is identical with the London edition (Jonathan Cape, 1976).
4. See Elizabeth Perkins, "Escape with a Convict: Patrick White's 'A Fringe of Leaves.'" *Meanjin Quarterly* 36, no. 2 (1977): 265–69. See also Jill Ward, "Patrick White's *A Fringe of Leaves*: History and Fiction," *Australian Literary Studies* 8, no. 3 (1978):402–18.
5. "Patrick White Speaks on Factual Writing and Fiction," *Australian Literary Studies* 10, no. 1 (1981):100–101.
6. Walsh, *Patrick White's Fiction*, p. 125. Walsh is referring to the special kind of religious emphasis he finds in the novel.
7. Katharine Prichard, *Coonardoo* (New York: W. W. Norton, 1930).
8. See A. Grove Day, *Eleanor Dark* (Boston: Twayne Publishers, 1976). Day stresses Dark's nationalism, liberalism, and integrity.
9. All page references here in parentheses are to *Big Toys* (Sydney, 1978). This quotation occurs on p. viii.
10. *The Night the Prowler: Short Story and Screen Play* (Ringwood, Victoria, 1978).
11. *The Twyborn Affair* (New York, 1980), p. 13; hereafter page references are cited in parentheses in the text.
12. William Walsh, "Centres of the Self," *Times Literary Supplement* (London), Nov. 30, 1979, p. 77.
13. Benjamin DeMott, "The Perils of Protean Man," *New York Times Book Review*, April 27, 1980, p. 3 and p. 32.
14. Walter Clemons, "Thrice-Born Hero," *Newsweek*, April 7, 1980, p. 90F.
15. Nicholas Mosley, "Seeing it Whole," *The Listener*, Nov. 29, 1979, pp. 761–62. See also Tom Paulin, "The Fire-Monster,"

Encounter (London) 54 (Jan. 1980):58–60. Paulin is "dismayed by the embittered silliness of *The Twyborn Affair*."

16. *Flaws in the Glass*, p. 145.

17. See Patrick White, "Flaws in the glass[:] Sketches for a self-portrait," *The Bulletin*, Jan. 29, 1980, pp. 146–54. The quotation appears on p. 151. The passage, slightly extended—and corrected—appears in the book-length autobiography. There White changed the phrase "overreaching grandeur" to "a grandeur too overwhelming to express." He—or his editor—also deleted the comma following the question mark. See *Flaws in the Glass*, p. 70.

18. *Flaws in the Glass*, pp. 80–81. Subsequent page references are indicated in parentheses.

Selected Bibliography

The various paperback reprints of many of White's novels, such as the Avon series in the United States and Penguin Books in England and Australia, are not listed here because they are not dependably available.

PRIMARY SOURCES

The Aunt's Story. London: Routledge, 1948; New York: Viking, 1948; London: Eyre & Spottiswoode, 1958.
Big Toys. Sydney: Currency Press, 1978.
The Burnt Ones. London: Eyre & Spottiswoode, 1964; New York: Viking, 1964.
The Cockatoos. London: Jonathan Cape, 1974; New York: Viking, 1975.
The Eye of the Storm. London: Jonathan Cape, 1973; New York: Viking, 1974.
Flaws in the Glass. London: Jonathan Cape, 1981; New York: Viking, 1981.
Four Plays. London: Eyre & Spottiswoode, 1965; New York: Viking, 1966.
A Fringe of Leaves. London: Jonathan Cape, 1976; New York: Viking, 1976.
Happy Valley. London: George C. Harap, 1939; New York, Viking, 1940.
The Living and the Dead. London: Routledge, 1941; New York: Viking, 1941; London: Eyre & Spottiswoode, 1962.
The Night the Prowler. London: Jonathan Cape, 1978; Ringwood, Victoria: Penguin Books Australia and Jonathan Cape, 1978.
The Ploughman and Other Poems. Sydney: Beacon Press, 1935.
"The Prodigal Son." *Australian Letters* 1, no. 3 (1958): 37–40.
Riders in the Chariot. London: Eyre & Spottiswoode, 1961; New York: Viking, 1961.
The Solid Mandala. London: Eyre & Spottiswoode, 1966; New York: Viking, 1966.
The Tree of Man. London: Eyre & Spottiswoode, 1956; New York: Viking, 1955.

The Twyborn Affair. London: Jonathan Cape, 1979; New York: Viking, 1980.

The Vivisector. London: Jonathan Cape, 1970; New York: Viking, 1970.

Voss. London: Eyre & Spottiswoode, 1957; New York: Viking, 1957; London: Longmans, Green, 1965.

SECONDARY SOURCES

Argyle, Barry. *Patrick White*. New York: Barnes & Noble, 1967. This well-meant tribute to White contains a few factual errors but also some provocative disagreements with other critics.

Beatson, Peter. *The Eye in the Mandala. Patrick White: A Vision of Man and God*. London: Paul Elek, 1976. This is a sincere and intelligently planned explication of White as essentially a mystic.

Björksten, Ingmar. *Patrick White: A General Introduction*. Translated by Stanley Gerson. St. Lucia, Queensland: University of Queensland Press, 1976. Published originally in 1973, this study of White's plays and fiction includes an interview with White not available elsewhere.

Blake, J. L. *Australian Writers*. Adelaide: Rigby, 1977. In this survey (through the late 1960s) the author relates White to both Thomas Hardy and Virginia Woolf and thus rescues him from Commonwealth crudities.

Brissenden, R. F. *Patrick White*. London: Longmans, Green, 1966. This early monograph in the series *Writers and Their Work* introduced White with enthusiasm and perceptiveness.

Colmer, John. *Patrick White's 'Riders in the Chariot.'* Melbourne: Edward Arnold, 1978. In this scholarly and conscientious study Professor Colmer explores "White's affinities with the medieval mind" insofar as the novelist tries to "draw the whole of human existence into unity."

Dutton, Geoffrey. *Patrick White*. Melbourne: Landsdowne Press, 1963. In this third revision of his essay on White, Dutton reveals the respect and concern for White's commitment that is typical of those who "found" the writer before the Nobel Prize made him famous. (A fourth revision of this work was published in 1973.)

Dyce, J. R. *Patrick White as Playwright*. St. Lucia: University of Queensland Press, 1974. In this scholarly study of White's early and mature dramas, Dyce reports what is not available as well as reproducing some rare documents, such as theater programs.

Herring, Thelma, and **Wilkes, G. A.** "A Conversation with Patrick White." *Southerly* 33, no. 2 (1973):132–43. One of the few personal interviews: White summarizes the facts about his schooling, early years as a jackeroo, apprentice playwright, and novelist. Importantly, White at that time identified all of his novels as "ironic" and also as "quite old-fashioned and traditional."

Kiernan, Brian. *Patrick White.* New York: St. Martin's Press, 1980. Although Kiernan did not have the advantage of White's latest works, *Flaws in the Glass* and *The Twyborn Affair*, his study is perceptive, well-documented, and less contentious than most.

Kippax, H. G. Introduction to *Four Plays by Patrick White.* Melbourne: Sun Books, 1967. Of special value for the introduction in which Kippax recapitulates the events associated with the production of the four plays.

Lawson, Alan. *Patrick White. (Australian Bibliographies.)* Melbourne: Oxford University Press, 1974. This is an inclusive and comprehensive bibliography of White's works, both major and minor, interviews, letters, and other artifacts as well as critical and bibliographical essays, through 1973.

———. "Unmerciful Dingoes? The Critical Reception of Patrick White." *Meanjin Quarterly* 32, no. 4 (1973):379–92. An important report and survey which corrects some of the legends about White's unpopularity at home. Lawson is obviously both dedicated and reliable as a witness.

Moore, T. Inglis. *Social Patterns in Australian Literature.* Berkeley and Los Angeles: University of California Press, 1971. The historian places White as part of a "revolutionary phenomenon," his novels having broken with the "social realists." White's influence on others has been "considerable."

Morley, Patricia. *The Mystery of Unity: Theme and Technique in the Novels of Patrick White.* Montreal and London: McGill-Queen's University Press, 1972. Morley gives "a prominent place to archetypal criticism." She frankly "places White's novels in a religious tradition" and "emphasizes the unity of vision which underlies all White's fiction."

Myers, David. *The Peacocks and the Bourgeoise.* Adelaide: Adelaide University Union Press, 1978. Subtitled "Ironic Vision in Patrick White's Shorter Prose Fiction," Myers's study emphasizes the affinities between the stories and the novels while probing the former for their own kind of evidence of the dualities in White's vision.

Semmler, Clement, ed. *Twentieth Century Australian Literary Criticism.* Melbourne: Oxford University Press, 1967. In addition to the essays on White by John McClaren and Sylvia Gzell, this collection is valuable for general studies of the genesis of modern Australian literature by dependable scholars such as Geoffrey Dutton, Vincent Buckley, and others.

Tacey, David. "Patrick White: Misconceptions about Jung's Influence." *American Literary Studies* 9, no. 2 (1979):245–46. A brief but cogent argument against overemphasizing Jung's influence on White: the "Unconscious" was not invented by Jung.

Thompson, John. "Australia's White Policy." *Australian Letters* 1, no. 3 (1958):42–45. A summing up in 1958 of the history of hostile reactions in Australia toward White and enthusiastic ones in England and the United States.

Walsh, William. *Patrick White's Fiction.* London: George Allen & Unwin, 1977. A must for any student of White's works. Walsh's dedication is not a detriment to his criticism, for unlike Morley and Beatson he does not have to prove a thesis.

Ward, Russel. *The History of Australia: The Twentieth Century.* New York: Harper & Row, 1977. The historian pursues the theme of an emerging national consciousness, citing the return of expatriate artists such as Patrick White as evidence of a maturing culture.

Whitman, Robert. "The Dream Plays of Patrick White." *Texas Studies in Literature and Language* 21, no. 2 (1979):240–59. The author takes White's dramas quite seriously and finds many similarities between his "thinking" and that of Strindberg. (This whole issue of the periodical is devoted to careful studies of White's writings.)

Wilkes, G. A., ed. *Ten Essays on Patrick White Selected from Southerly* (1964–67). Sydney: Angus & Robertson, 1970. Marking the advent of serious scholarship related to the pre-Nobel enthusiasm for White, this collection of essays is still viable.

Wilkes, G. A., and **Reid, J. C.** *The Literatures of the British Commonwealth: Australia and New Zealand.* Edited by A. L. McLeod. University Park: Pennsylvania State University Press, 1970. The section on Australian literature by G. A. Wilkes is especially pertinent to White's work.

Index